EVERY GIRL'S DUTY

ALICE CATHERINE MILES

Every Girl's Duty

THE DIARY OF A VICTORIAN DEBUTANTE

———

Edited with a Commentary by
Maggy Parsons

ANDRE DEUTSCH

FIRST PUBLISHED 1992 BY
ANDRE DEUTSCH LIMITED
105-106 GREAT RUSSELL STREET, LONDON WC1B 3LJ
COPYRIGHT © 1992 BY MAGGY PARSONS
ALL RIGHTS RESERVED

British Library Cataloguing in Publication Data
Every girl's duty: the diary of a Victorian
debutante.
I. Parsons, Maggy
942.081092

ISBN 0 233 98755 X

Printed in Great Britain by
St. Edmundsbury Press, Bury St. Edmunds
Suffolk

"I consider it every girl's duty
to marry £80,000 a year" –
Alice Catherine Miles, aged seventeen

Contents

ACKNOWLEDGEMENTS

Perhaps the easiest way for me to acknowledge with gratitude my debts to those who have helped towards making this book is to mention them as they came on the scene during its progress. Before it began, Mr Bryan Gipps had kindly lent to me, on several occasions, the diaries of his deceased great-grandmother Mrs Louisa Thomas of Hollingbourne. Mrs Irene Newbury of Hollingbourne gave me Duppa papers acquired by her late husband, amongst which were Alice's diaries. Hints in these papers sent me off to Ayot St Lawrence, where I was directed to Mrs Harding, a village resident, who had some recollections of Alice and her daughters; and to Mr and Mrs Jury, custodians of the National Trust property "Shaw's Corner". In Ayot I met Mrs Chloe Willing, who gave me much time and assistance, and later lent me a diary for 1908 of Alice's son Lionel. Mrs Willing enabled me to find Mrs Monica Ames, widow of Lionel, then over ninety, and now, sadly, deceased. This lady, then living in Bridport, mentioned two other relatives, Mr Ian Shield and Mrs Diana Knight, each of whom I visited and from whom I received much information and the happy experience of seeing photographs and pictures relating to Alice and her family. Special thanks are due to Mr Shield, whose great generosity in lending the albums has contributed so much to this volume.

The staff of Avon County Libraries were most helpful in providing material about Leigh Court, and the staff of Newark and Sherwood District Council allowed me to see Kelham Hall and provided information. Kent County Council's Archives Office gave me access to other Duppa papers.

Miss Rosina Dalziell helped with the typing, and without Mrs Inge Hack's enlightenment on German *Schrift* parts of the diary would have remained indecipherable. Dr Martin Moss gave some medical advice, and Mrs Kathleen Jannaway helped to elucidate the complications of French. Ian Talboys was responsible for excellent photographic work.

I owe much to Elwyn Evans who has advised, encouraged and assisted throughout, and has acted as chauffeur, copy checker, research assistant, and, not least, subsidiser of a voracious typewriter with a large appetite for tapes and paper.

I found useful and interesting information in the following works: *Culture and Society in France, 1848–1898*, by Professor F. W. J.

Acknowledgments

Hemmings (Batsford); *Edward VII, Prince and King*, by Giles St Aubyn (Collins); *Lady Colin Campbell — Victorian "Sex Goddess"*, by G. H. Fleming (Windrush Press); *The Mitford Family Album*, by Sophia Murphy (Sidgwick & Jackson); and *Bernard Shaw, Collected Letters 1911–1925*, Edited by Dan H. Laurence (Max Reinhardt), from which the GBS letter on page 172 is taken.

Finally I offer grateful thanks to my publishers, in particular to Esther Whitby and Diana Athill, whose enthusiasm, encouragement and guidance brought to practical reality a long-cherished aspiration.

Maggy Parsons

THE ILLUSTRATIONS

All the family pictures came from family photograph albums, kindly lent by Alice's grandson, Mr Ian Shield. Bristol Public Library supplied the drawing of Leigh Court (from vol. xxx of The Brackenridge Collection). The Mansell Collection supplied the caricature of Lord Harrington by Lib, and those of Tommy Bowles and Sir Francis Knollys by Spy. The Mary Evans Picture Library found for us the Victorian engravings reproduced at the start of each chapter, as well as the ornamental surround incorporated into the jacket design. Thanks are also due to the National Portrait Gallery, for the portrait of Frederick Burnaby by James Tissot and that of Lady Colin Campbell by Giovanni Boldini, as well as for the caricature of the 5th Marquess of Lansdowne; to the Réunion des Musées Nationaux, Paris, for the watercolour of a soirée at the Tuileries by Henri Baron; to the RIBA Drawings Collection for the architect's elevation of Kelham Hall; and to the Trustees of the Wallace Collection, London, for their permission to reproduce the painting "Psyche" by Jean-Baptiste Greuze.

Discovering a Diary

IT must often be that the discovery, deciphering and publication of a diary arise from fortunate and unforeseen chance, and the present case is no exception.

Newcomers to an attractive village are often eager to explore the settlement's past and its place in the history of the county or the nation. Even a casual visitor will wander round the parish church, gaze at the memorials and speculate about the people whose lives are commemorated. Where a village has no published history, the newcomer may spend happy hours consulting the parish register and the county archives, or deciphering gravestones, or working out the heraldic devices in the stained-glass windows. Slowly the jigsaw puzzle of the village's history is fitted together. There will always be gaps, but against that there is always the chance of some new scrap coming to light: one can never be certain that the picture is finished.

My associate and partner Elwyn Evans and I had become addicted to this pursuit, although our interests lay in rather different areas. We had both assisted with exhibitions of local history in the village of Hollingbourne, in Kent, where we live, and had both contributed to a Village Quarterly, which I originated in 1978, and continue to edit. In the course of these activities we had become involved — as so many people do, in so many villages — in attempts to raise funds for the restoration of the church. It was suggested that one of these should be a *Son et Lumière* production in the church; and although, as it happened, this came to nothing, it did lead Elwyn Evans to begin a detailed study of the Duppa family of Hollingbourne, his starting point being the memorials in the church. He collected an immense amount of material, and his interest in the Duppas caused many people to produce memories, letters, diaries, books, pictures and other references which shed light on a family previously obscure — to us,

1

that is: we were to discover several "Duppa students" scattered round the world, as well as Duppa descendants.

The most valuable find occurred after the sudden and untimely death of a local antiquarian and numismatist, Mr V. J. (Nicky) Newbury, who, with his wife, was well-known as a collector of all kinds of antiquities. Mr Newbury had rescued from a local farmer many boxes of family papers belonging to the Duppas, and these had for some years been kept in his attic, awaiting examination before they were despatched to the County Archive. Mrs Newbury, after her husband's death, began exploring the attic, discovered the papers, and kindly offered to show them to us.

The contents of the several large boxes were brittle, stained and dirty. Bundles of legal papers were tied with pink tape or with string, and roughly wrapped in dusty brown paper. There were copies of wills sealed with great blobs of red wax; there were beautifully calligraphed title deeds and conveyances of land, expressed in obscure legal jargon and innocent of punctuation; there were scraps of undated letters, household accounts and bills. Finally there was a collection of well-bound notebooks of varying size, most of them filled from cover to cover with writing which was bold and vigorous, though changing in size and style so that at first sight it might have been by more than one hand.

Elwyn sat in one room surrounded by piles of grubby papers, endeavouring to sort them into some kind of order. I took the notebooks, one after another as he discovered them, into another room (rather as a woodmouse carries edible treasure off to its hole) and began to read them — with difficulty, but with increasing astonishment and amusement. They were diaries, written not by any Duppa but by a girl, apparently quite young, called Alice Catherine Miles. The revelations, the humour, the sheer outrageousness of what I found — I kept running back to Elwyn to read bits out to him — kept us up till nearly two o'clock in the morning.

Closer inspection over some weeks revealed that only three of the volumes were diaries: a bound notebook covering the period June 20th 1868 to September 1868; a second bound volume running from September 14th 1868 to August 1869; and a coverless, perhaps home-made notebook made from folded writing paper, which ran from August 14th 1869 to June 12th 1870. In addition there were four books of notes of sermons, two of short essays, three of accounts of charitable disbursements, and one bound volume of short literary extracts, in French and in English: a "commonplace book" such as young ladies often made, this one with the added interest of containing a few original pieces written by the compiler, "A. C. Miles".

A more thorough study of the diaries soon revealed them to be vivid portrayals of French society under the Second Empire, and of London society in the same period, the scene observed by a lively and intelligent, though immature, mind which was very much the product of those societies. Fluent, copious, written at speed (sometimes as dawn broke after a ball), they revealed the writer as a sharp observer, with a fair bump of conceit and a vivid imagination: in particular the latter, for some of the incidents and especially some of the conversations gave the impression of being largely fictitious.

Transcribing the diaries was to prove far from easy. By and large Alice's handwriting is well formed even at speed, but the quality of pens and ink varied. Occasionally, too, she deleted names or phrases either by thickly inking them over or by scratching them out with a knife. Later, with the help of the context, I could sometimes make out the hidden name, but sometimes it is gone for good. In a few places she had cut out whole pages, leaving us forever in the dark at some highly critical points of her emotional journey.

What at first seemed an insuperable difficulty was eventually overcome: many pages were written in an obscure script which for some time remained baffling. At last I realised that certain words appeared to contain a "u", recognisable as such by the presence of a German accent or mark placed over it. Having therefore conjectured that it might be German *Schrift*, or cursive hand, I consulted a German-born friend who kindly wrote out for me the *Schrift* alphabet. Even with that help I was able, at first, only to worry out the occasional word and guess others, but gradually it became easier until at last I could transliterate, and so read, entire sections. What Alice had done was to write in English but use *Schrift*: a clever trick, and her fluency in the *Schrift* was impressive.

She used many French words and phrases (not italicised in the text, because of the ease with which Alice moved between the languages). My own French is of the schoolroom kind, so although much of Alice's can easily be understood from the context, I had to keep a dictionary at my elbow. When it came to preparing the diary for publication it was decided that, for the sake of readers at my own level in the language, footnote translations of all but the most obvious things would be added.

At the same stage the decision was made to keep Alice's punctuation and grammar, but to correct her spelling. It is better than most people's, so her occasional carelessness is irritating rather than charmingly comic, like that of Daisy Ashford in *The Young Visiters*.

Another, and more important, decision taken at this stage was to make cuts[1]. From the London diary the only omissions are a few short garbled passages where haste and/or fatigue had destroyed the sense, or where an óblique reference to something which Alice had recorded in the pages which she herself had excised was beyond interpretation. Later, when she was staying in Ireland or was back in France, cuts were made when it was felt that repetition was becoming boring. Alice herself was often bored in those places (particularly in Paris), which may explain a slightly weary feeling of "Here we go again!" as she embarked on yet another idle flirtation.

With one exception, nothing that was important to Alice, and thus to us, has been cut. The exception is a story she recounted to her friend Jeanne and recorded in the diary, obviously because she was proud of it: she had turned it into a literary exercise of some length. The nugget of information it contained is of great interest — see page 95 — but the style became heavily self-conscious and — alas — tedious: too much so to be worth preserving in print, or so I felt.

ALICE'S ANTECEDENTS

Alice's beautiful mother (there is plenty of evidence for her beauty) was born Francis Elizabeth Roche, between 1825 and 1830. Her family belonged to the Anglo-Irish gentry, and their home was at, or near, Carass, Co. Limerick. According to *A Genealogical and Heraldic Dictionary of the Peerage and Baronetage of the British Empire* by John Burke (1842), they had been settled there since the fifteenth century. Their crest included a roach, and their motto was *"Dieu est ma Roche"*. As Alice's mother floats in and out of her daughter's diary she leaves an impression of frivolity, considerable ambition, and not wholly unexceptionable morals.

The Miles family originated in the west of England and spread to Barbados and Jamaica during the seventeenth century, when fortunes were being made from sugar. From 1752 to about 1890 they owned

[1]The original document is with Maggie Parsons, who can be contacted through the publisher.

two banks in Bristol, which were eventually incorporated into the National Westminster.

Alice's great-great-grandfather, William Miles, was born in Ledbury, Herefordshire, made his money in Jamaica, then returned to Bristol in 1766 to set up as a merchant: a Miles fleet traded with New Zealand and Australia throughout the 1800s. William's son, Philip John (1773–1845) acquired and rebuilt Leigh Court, which became the home of the branch of the family to which Alice belonged. Descendants of Philip John's second marriage lived not far away at Kings Weston. Philip John's son William, Alice's grandfather, was educated at Eton and Christchurch, Oxford. He was thrice a Member of Parliament, was a partner in the Miles bank and was created 1st baronet in 1859. He had twelve children in addition to Alice's father – another Philip John who became 2nd baronet in 1878. This huge family was probably the reason why the Mileses we get to know in the diary felt short of money while waiting to inherit the family seat and the title, and why Alice knew that in spite of the family's general prosperity she must rely on her charm rather than on a handsome dowry to win her a husband.

SETTING THE STAGE

Since the defeat of Napoleon I by the British in 1815, France and Britain had existed in an uneasy but close relationship. The alternations of Empire, Monarchy and Republic in France need not detain us, but in 1848, the year of Philip Miles's marriage to Frances Elizabeth Roche, the King of France, Louis Philippe, was ousted by the republican element and fled to England. Napoleon Bonaparte's nephew became President of the Republic, and in 1852 assumed the title of Emperor: Napoleon III. The Second Empire began.

Socially this was an ostentatious and luxurious period, which saw the continuation of the interrupted rebuilding of Paris on spectacular lines, largely by the famous Haussmann, and was notable for extravagance of dress, lavish entertainments and high spending by the rich, led by the glamorous Empress Eugénie. While the poor festered and boiled in the slums, the rich middle and upper classes showed off their magnificent carriages in the Bois, sailed their yachts off Boulogne and Dieppe, dined at expensive restaurants, went to balls at the Tuileries palace, and vied with each other in dress and jewellery at the opera, the theatres, concerts and receptions. They duelled, gambled, flirted and intrigued; acted in extravagant amateur theatricals and read daring novels, apparently unaware of the repeated earthquake-tremors which threatened further serious eruptions. France's serious writers and thinkers were often subjected to a vigorous, if unpredictable censorship, while the spurious, sentimental and prurient flourished. Professor F.W.J. Hemmings has remarked that the Second Empire was "stuffy and gay by turns" and "couldn't make up its mind whether it preferred to be titillated or bored".

The British Court, under the stern moral guidance of Queen Victoria and her incorruptible consort Albert, was very different: all was moral uplift, industry, religious observance and high seriousness. Albert Edward, Prince of Wales, was just about beginning to break the bonds of his strict upbringing when the death of his father plunged the Court into a gloom of mourning that was to last for over twenty years. But outside the Court high society in Britain differed little in its behaviour from that in France — and as soon as he reached man's estate the Prince of Wales participated to the full in its extravagance and frivolity. Despite the variable political climate, society in France and England seems to have been almost interchangeable. In the 1850s the Empress Eugénie and Queen Victoria exchanged visits (Queen Victoria recorded in her diary that the Empress was "very ladylike") and the Prince of Wales's love of France seems to have sprung from his youthful enjoyment of a Court more relaxed and friendly than the one he was used to. Many Britons, especially eldest sons waiting to inherit the family fortune, and younger ones with less to look forward to, found living in France a good deal cheaper than in England. When the Franco-Prussian war broke out in 1870 they fled back home in droves, but they returned to France as soon as they could afterwards.

The Emperor and Empress also fled, never to return, and spent the rest of their days in leafy Chislehurst in Kent.

Mr and Mrs Miles, with Alice and their younger daughters, were among the many English people who had made their homes in Paris, because they could afford a better style of living there than they would be able to enjoy in England until Philip Miles came into his baronetcy and his estate. The paintings of Winterhalter, Tissot, Frith and many others show us how their world looked: Alice, in her own vivid, flippant style, tells us much of how it felt.

PART ONE

The Diary

The London Season, 1868

LICE embarked on her first London Season with a good deal less formality than was customary. Indeed, she seems to have slipped into it almost by accident. She was without benefit of a launching through the ritual of presentation to Her Majesty at one of the Queen's "Drawing Rooms", and it is obvious that her mother had neglected to establish the proper network of connections with suitable hostesses which would ensure her girl all the right invitations. As will be seen, the Mileses knew, if not "everybody", at least a great many very grand people; but they do not seem always to have known them in quite the right way.

Alice, nevertheless, was plunged into the feverish round of calls, balls, dinners, soirées, theatres, rides and drives that the Season entailed.

The exacting régime was along the following lines. A late start in the morning allowed time for little more than recovery from the previous evening's exertions, and repairs to toilette and complexion.

Luncheon might be taken at home, or with friends, and was as nearly informal as the manners of the age allowed. In the afternoon, one might drive or stroll in one of the royal parks (usually Hyde Park), or, if rich, confident and attractive enough, ride in Rotten Row. Always, of course, there were chaperones. So-called "morning calls" occurred in the early afternoon, involving an extraordinarily ceremonious exchange of calling cards. Later calls, the Five o'clock Tea, were more relaxed and Alice comments that it was her own rule to "go to dress" at 6.15 p.m. This seems ridiculously early, if dinner were not till eight or nine, but dinner was the most serious and formal part of the day, dress was immensely elaborate, and Alice, in order to create the impression she was determined on, had to make lengthy preparations of toilette and coiffure. Her nimble-fingered and long-suffering maid Zéphine (short for Josephine perhaps) must have found her an exacting mistress, to judge by the accounts Alice gives of her flower-bedecked dresses.

A formal dinner was lengthy and ruled by an exacting protocol. Seating and the procession from the drawing room to the dining room had to be arranged by the hosts with the strictest regard to social status and convention. The elaborately set and decorated tables groaned under successive gargantuan courses, which, fortunately, were not all obligatory. At a given signal, the ladies returned to the drawing room, leaving the gentlemen to alcohol, smoking, risqué stories, business deals and political discussion.

Eventually they joined the ladies in the drawing room and the evening would continue with card games, conversation (that is, gossip), a little music and, in Alice's and many another's case, flirtation. Alternatively, instead of a formal evening in the house, one might proceed to a play, opera or concert, not primarily to hear the performance but to meet friends, catch up on gossip, and to see and be seen – and to observe who was wearing what, or who was with whom.

Late though it was, one might then proceed to a ball. It was not uncommon to arrive at midnight and continue till four or five o'clock in the morning. Small wonder that after three weeks of this Alice was nearing collapse.

The Season coincided with the Parliamentary recess, lasting from Easter to August. The succession of race meetings, river parties, regattas and picnics faded off into visits to the country houses of friends or relations. Cowes Week in August, frequented by the really rich, happy and glorious, led by HRH the Prince of Wales, was followed by the "sporting" season, where on country estates selected kinds of furry or feathered creature were massacred in hundreds of thousands by all males with any pretension to gentility or wealth.

London, Saturday June 20th, 1868

We arrived, Father and I, after the most fatiguing journey, long sea route, a bad day, an indifferent passage and every other calamity unhappy travellers are subjected to in the normal course of events; and I wondered very much as I curled myself comfortably up in bed, in a room of decent size, and in every respect different to Paris, how I shall like my stay here? I was threatened first with Dover, when Augustus Lumley interposed like some guardian angel and offered us his house, for the remaining 3 weeks of the season: how shall I like it? I sleepily asked myself again, half opening my eyes to assure myself of the blessed fact that I had indeed escaped from tiny Rue des Ecuries d'Artois[1] for some time at least. The season in Paris bored me to extinction, though I had everything as completely my own way as the proverbial bull in the china shop, was the acknowledged belle (I don't see why I should pretend to ignore it vis à vis de mon livre)[2], and had paragraphs respecting my fair face and beautiful toilettes inserted in more newspapers than I should care to count — and yet — I was bored, wearied with it all, and cried every now and then from sheer dullness, without being in the least able to explain why; but however that doesn't matter; being a young and pretty woman I have a perfect right to indulge in as many caprices, and be in every way as illogical as I please — with which sage reflection I think I shall go to sleep, and leave to time to prove if London gaiety suits my moral temperament, or whether after trying it in the balance I shall find it as utterly wanting in every interesting element, as I did the French capital and its inmates.

[1]The Miles's Paris house, so much resented by Alice, sounds as though it were in a mews.
[2]So far as my diary is concerned.

Alice does not often call Philip John Miles "Father". Usually he is "the Dear Boy". Some of the people she calls "cousin", including Augustus Lumley, seem to have been fairly distant relations (though her family tree – page 178 – shows she could have had dozens of close ones). The amiable and useful Augustus was perhaps related to the Earl of Scarborough – the Scarborough family name is Lumley. He had, at any rate, entrée into the best society and a house in fashionable Eaton Place – just what Alice needed. Whether he was a bachelor or a widower we do not know – if a widower, clearly quite a merry one. He never reappears in the diary after the end of this stay in London, which seems odd considering the degree of friendship implied. One hopes that friendship did not come to an unhappy end during the "family row" which will occur just before the Mileses depart for Ireland on July 18th: an event so disagreeable that it will cause Alice to excise nine pages from her diary.

Saturday June 27th

Well, I have had a week of this London life, and up to the present I am not disappointed, it is all very new and strange but on the whole I like it. Sunday we went to the Zoological Gardens, and excited considerably more interest than the animals with our Parisienne toilettes and Parisienne good looks. May Manners Sutton[1], one of the richest and naughtiest of London Grandes Dames, is our great card here; she is rather jealous of Mother who was guilty of the enormous indiscretion of putting her into the shade at Lords[2] the other day, but I am with her constantly, as she imagines I draw the men, and don't take possession of them when they arrive. She has always a certain Miss Edith Wood in her pocket also, the most un-clerical daughter of a respectable clergyman, the prettiest little golden-haired blue-eyed doll imaginable, immensely amusing but without sufficient savoir-faire to play her cards to advantage; intensely fast, and not clever enough to conceal it. She flirts very considerably with May's brother, a great big overgrown unhealthy-looking Blue, Fred Burnaby by name: and May on her side occupies herself much more than the individual's merits seem to me to warrant about Edith's cousin, Baby Stewart (not the genuine "Baby" of the Guards, but his youngest

[1]Another "cousin" – exact relationship unknown.
[2]Perhaps at the Eton and Harrow cricket match – an important social event.

brother Robert), a plain puny little child barely one-and-twenty, with all the exigencies and tempers of a fractious infant joined to the jealousy and imbecility of a man. However, such as he is, he finds favour in May's eyes, and she will not hear a word against him — How long will the fancy last? — Three weeks at the outside.

I lunch at her house nearly every day, discuss philosophical nonsense and the last on dits with Edith and Henan [?], (Captain Burnaby's nom de guerre), and amuse myself watching the progress of May's little game. I turned round the other day just at the very moment I ought not, and caught her giving "Baby" a kiss that was the reverse of motherly — Really for a woman of her age, she is the greatest idiot of my acquaintance.

Frederick Gustavus Burnaby (1842—1885) of the Royal Horse Guards was to achieve fame by crossing Russian Asia on horseback, a feat described in his *Ride to Khiva* (recently republished by Century). He acted as correspondent for *The Times*, went to Khartoum to investigate General Gordon's expedition, made several balloon ascents, and was killed in action at Abu Klea. His portrait by Tissot — a wonderfully evocative work — is in the National Portrait Gallery.

To come back to my own affairs, Cocky[1] who appreciated our company in Paris called three times this week; I had the bad luck to be at May's the first two visits, but the third time he came by appointment, asked in an innocent manner if Mother was in, when he knew perfectly well she was out having spoken to her in Berkeley Square: came up the stairs and sat and stared at me for two mortal hours, saying nothing which admitted of the faintest pleasant construction. — I don't the least dispute that in my cool white muslin and lace and profusion of pink ribbons, I was quite entitled to all the attention he gave me, but still I think he might have talked a little at the same time, and not left all the conversation to me, which in this tropical heat is too much of an exertion — When he was gone, I issued a "not at home" for future visitors and laid [sic] quite still on the sofa till dinnertime, fearing an extinction de voix or some other untoward result, arising from such an unusual exertion.

[1]The nickname of Lord Lansdowne, of whom more later.

Every Girl's Duty

Oh dear! Oh dear! I am so angry I don't know what to do. A message has just come to say that my great-grandfather's second wife has been gathered to her forefathers at the ripe age of 76, and we are all to be plunged into desolation and mourning for an indefinite period. Mother declares we shall go out just the same, but still all our pretty dresses must be put in the cupboard, and we must assume mourning garments at total variance with our feelings on the subject.

Oh dear me! What a blessed thing it would be if one had no relations. As far as my experience of them goes, they do nothing but worry and contradict you during their lives and at their death plunge you into hot black garments when the thermometer is a 100 and something in the shade, all human nature disporting itself in butterfly radiance.

To end all, Mother came to say I must attend a solemn family dinner at my grandfather's instead of the merry little party we were to have at May's — But Providence spared me this last trial, and I was left to get used to my grief with the M. Suttons. We went to see some Japanese jugglers during the evening, and wound up with ——[2] which of course was highly incorrect, and as such extremely diverting.

*   *   *   *   *

Isn't it an extraordinary thing that everybody's particular business in this world seems to be to neglect their own, that they may the better interfere with their neighbours'? — Father has been congratulated several times on my engagement to Cocky, and this morning in the Park several people began at me, and all this on the strength of our harmless rides in Paris: what on earth would the busy bodies say if they heard of his three visits this week and some little parisian details! — It is a great bore because I shall have to avoid the poor young man in public, for though he pleases me immensely, and the envious glances cast on me by young ladies "on their promotion" amuse me still more, still I cannot afford to have it said I am his Lordship's property, and thus keep off the other men; in favour of one who, however galling it may be to my vanity to confess it, means nothing in the world but amusing himself as long as the fancy lasts.

*   *   *   *   *

[1]Alice's asterisks indicate a shift of subject or passing of time.
[2]Alice often substitutes dashes for names. When I have identified the person I insert the name.

I missed so many people by so doing that I have given up going to the Park with May and Edith of an afternoon, and sit at home for any visitors that come, instead. Augustus keeps me company for he has taken it into his head to paint me, and is doing the sweetest Greuze head imaginable, all my hair down simply kept back from the face by a blue ribbon. Visitors are shewn into the painting room, or else I go into the drawing room to them: selon la personne qui vient[1]. The way they appreciate the artistic negligence of my appearance, my transparent muslins and flowing hair is something wonderful — What a different life to Paris to be sure and how I enjoy it! —

People often said that Alice was like a painting by Jean-Baptiste Greuze (1725—1805), who began by painting popular *genre* scenes, portraits and studies of children, fell out of fashion, and attempted to redeem his fortunes by producing what the *Penguin History of Art* describes as "titillating semi-draped figures of young girls . . . of mawkish sentimentality", sometimes titled as virtues or moods. These were much to the taste of Alice's day, and also of Alice herself. There are one or two of his pictures in the National Portrait Gallery and many in the Wallace Collection.

Monday 29 June

While Augustus and I were painting today in came a certain Sir Samuel Hayes with an invitation for me for his grandmother Lady Pakenham's ball tonight. The way he stood motionless and stared at my hair was something fine to see. He was so struck dumb with admiration that he could not even bring out a compliment. An occasional "Oh my God" was the only vent it found in words. He looked so absurdly ugly too, with his amazed countenance, rolling his eyes at me from the other side of the room, that it required all my good breeding to prevent me from bursting out laughing.

I enjoyed myself very much at this ball, where I made my entrée into London Society in spite of my being on the qui vive for Cocky all the evening, who was unable to come as he promised, being kept discussing the Irish Church[2] in the House of Lords till 3 o'clock in the

[1]Selon la personne . . . Depending on who it is.
[2]The Anglican Church in Ireland was finally disestablished a year later, in 1869, as part of Gladstone's attempt to solve the "Irish Question."

morning: I began to feel quite an enmity to that same House of Lords and the Commanders of the British Army, as the men I want are always sure to be ordered on duty by either the one or the other, just at the time I require them and their services. I did not break my heart however, about Cocky's non-arrival, his contemporaries took very good care that I should have small time to miss him. Augustus introduced me to every man worth knowing in the room, and I was agreeably surprised at finding myself to the full as much admired as I had been in Paris, which, to tell the truth, I had never ventured to expect. Before introducing anyone Augustus gave me a rapidly whispered enumeration of their possessions and social standing: for instance —

"Beauty Campbell, Captain, Guards, splendid place in the North, £20,000 a year:
　　　　— Captain Campbell —
　　　　Miss Miles."

It was very difficult not to laugh, with the individual standing unconsciously opposite you; and this individual, Beauty Campbell, so called from being one of the best-looking men in the service, was indeed a splendid specimen: his six-foot-three, dark brown hair, frank open face and large violet eyes with the long dark lashes, were perfectly refreshing after the puny dark-browed frenchmen, with whom my craving after beauty had been put off up to the present. The more I see of my countrymen, the prouder I am of them, I never imagined there could be such lovely men. I did not think much of the women, they were mostly goodlooking, very badly dressed and entirely taken up with themselves and the effect they were or were not producing.

Watching them a certain portion of St James's epistle recurred most forcibly to my memory; stigmatising hearers and not doers of the word, the apostle says they are like "a man beholding his natural face in a glass, who having looked goeth his way and straightway forgetteth what manner of man he was" — surely no such slur could be cast on the vanity of 19th century belles.

* * * * *

Sir Samuel tried to inveigle me into a flirtation, but as I had previously ascertained he has only £4,000 a year which he has abandoned to his mother for the education of his eleven brothers and sisters, there would be no interested side in any such proceedings; and he is not sufficiently goodlooking to render [them?] interesting, and a flirtation devoid of either of these indispensible elements does not at all enter into my plan of action. I wound up the evening by a valse and petit souper with Beauty Campbell, though I was obliged to throw over Lord Down, a most uninteresting young nobleman with a large rent-roll, by so doing. While we were sitting trifling with chicken, pâté de fois gras, jellies and fruits, pour nous donner une contenance[1], doing very little in the way of eating and a great deal in talking, I amused myself relieving the dead white mourning of my dress with some of the crimson roses with which the table was strewn: having used or rejected all within my reach, I suggested to Beauty he should go and get me some more off a neighbouring table — but like most Guardsmen Beauty was averse to moving when he found himself in comfortable quarters, and he was too satisfied with his position just at present to be in any hurry to change it; so he called out to Sir Samuel who was passing — "I say Sammy, Miss Miles wants some of those roses, just bring over some, like a good fellow." Sir Samuel turned to the roses as desired, examined them with a critical eye and then remarking "They are all withered, but you shall have some tomorrow" — departed the way he had come in. So Beauty, sorely against his will had to bestir himself, pick me out two or three buds, then Father called me: so he put me into the carriage: and so home.

Tuesday 30th June

On coming home from the Park this morning, I found the most magnificent bouquet of roses heart could desire, waiting for me with Sir Samuel Hayes' compliments. That's what he meant, then, last night! What a very charming young man! I'm sure I wish I lived in a country where I am so well appreciated.

Friday 3rd July

I was sitting to Augustus in as fairy-like a costume of white and turquoise blue, as if Greatgrandmothers were a myth, and mourning for them a thing of the past; when Louisa came to tell me Sir Samuel Hayes was waiting in the drawing room. His delight when I came in with my hair down again was something comical. "May I kiss it?" he

[1]pour nous donner . . . to keep up appearances.

asked, taking up one long tress, and looking at it, as you may see a man look at a baby, or anything else of a tender description he doesn't understand. I gave the required permission; a very safe one, seeing it was a good yard from my face and he was as pleased as you might have expected him to be if the kiss had been bestowed on quite a different place — I don't think it was too much of a concession, considering the roses and all.

Notwithstanding his being in the Guards, the stupid fellow has not been able to procure me a ticket for the Blues' ball, which is to be Monday next. All London is frantic at not being able to get invitations, so of course my amour propre is touched, and whether I go or not, have a card I must and will, though how it is to be managed I don't quite see. I shall not fail anyhow for want of aiders and abetters, for Sammy, Beauty Campbell, Augustus, Fred Burnaby, Lansdowne, Lord Carrington, and last but not least HRH the Duke of Cambridge are all on the qui vive for a ticket for me too. When Sammy was gone, I went back to Augustus and the painting; but before he had done scolding me for such a long absence, the door opened, and his servant announcing "Mr Cornwallis West" in walked one of his particular artist friends, and uncommonly surprised he looked at seeing me, as you may easily imagine. I must own to a decided penchant towards these charming London men Fate has lately thrown me among, and when a little bit of an artist withal, they are perfectly irresistible. Besides, this particular specimen was six foot three, and uncommonly handsome, and evidently admired me to the full as much as I did him, so in five minutes we were chattering away gaily, the object of his visit being entirely forgotten, and Augustus in despair exclaiming "My dear little cousin, I don't mean to say but what you look perfectly bewitching, standing there with your face turned up to Cornwallis, and those sunbeams falling on your head like an aureole lighting up that mass of hair to a still deeper golden glory. But still, however becoming the effect may be in the abstract, if you would only return to your throne in the shade, and look at that Vandyke on the wall, instead of at Cornwallis, my picture would get along much faster from the change of position. West, my dear fellow, an artist yourself, you can understand my feelings: be kind enough to go and search out that tapestry you came for, and allow my fair model to return to her duties." Which at last the culprit reluctantly proceeded to do, after extorting a promise that I would come to the party he gives Monday night.

18

But the fates were averse to our painting in peace that day: I was very good for ten minutes after Mr West's departure, only obstinately refusing to issue a "not at home" for future visitors as Augustus required of me, and very lucky it was I didn't, for almost immediately afterwards Louisa came and informed me "If you please, Miss, the Marquis of Lansdowne is in the drawing room." Now I was much more in the humour for a flirtation with my faithless little admirer than for screwing my neck into elegant attitudes for Augustus; I went at once, telling him he might remain where he was till I called him, besides I wanted to hear the details of that Maidenhead expedition; also my glass and my previous visitor's eyes had informed me that I was looking my very best: a little fact that might have slightly influenced me also — Anyhow, go I did, and we were in the midst of a most animated conversation when I heard a most violent coup de sonnette. Now earlier in the day, when on coming in I had let down my hair and laid aside my gloomy mourning, for the dainty muslin and lace over blue silk I now wore, I gave Louisa strict orders to show any gentleman upstairs, but unless it was Mrs Manners Sutton, to tell any ladies I was out, which explains the amusing scene that took place downstairs whilst, unconscious of impending misfortune, Lansdowne and I continued our conversation in the drawing room. As soon as the door was opened in walked the most particular and strait-laced of all my insupportable relations — Aunt Agatha Somerset[1], accompanied by three children, two nurses and a perambulator. "Mrs Miles?" she asked in what was meant to be an imposing tone of voice. "Out" was the in every way truthful answer. "Mr Miles?" "Out." "And Miss Miles?" "Miss Miles is not at home either" replied Louisa readily, for though London and not Parisian bred, a very little tuition bestowed on her natural talents for intrigue would develop her into as perfect a soubrette as any Balzac's[2] pen has celebrated.

Then after these questions asked and answered, she (Louisa) still holding the door, looked enquiringly at Aunt Aggie and her interesting young family as if to ask what else was required. She was not long left in suspense, for, remarking she would go into the drawing room and write a note to me, my relative moved towards the stairs: here was a nice predicament, but it being evident to Louisa, she (Aunt Agatha)

[1] Alice's father's sister.
[2] Alice had at least a nodding acquaintance with a wide range of French writing, though Byron is the only English author she quotes from.

was a person I did not wish to receive, her ready wit did not forsake her. "I beg your pardon, Ma'am, if you will be kind enough to slip into the dining room, I will bring you paper, ink and pens." But Aunt Aggie, combining Louisa's empressement with Lord Lansdowne's neat equipage with its well-known coronet and prancing ponies drawn up most en evidence before the door, began to smell a rat, and was not to be so easily put off the scent. She waved poor Louisa majestically aside, "Young woman, I am going upstairs; come, children" and go upstairs she did, turning a very deaf ear to all remonstrations and, opening the drawing room door, sailed in, a rather uninteresting but virtuous picture of maternal felicity, in the midst of her young family all swaddled up to the eyes, be it remembered, in the deepest crêpe. Had she been in mourning for my shortcomings her woe could not have been more complete. What a sight met her eyes! There I was leaning back in the softest of easy chairs, playing with Sir Sammy's roses placed on the table by my side, my dishevelled hair falling over the cushion and my shoulders in the prettiest confusion, held back only by an azure ribbon matching the delicate tint of my dress: and above all, the greatest unpardonable sin of the whole deadly cata- . logue, there at my feet on a low chair, the effect I was producing on him written pretty plainly in his eyes, sat the Marquis of Lansdowne, the man she had been hunting ineffectually the whole season for her own daughter — and all of this when she, my father's own sister, had been denied me, told by that unblushing impudent hussy downstairs that I was out — Tableau! Imagine her face, across whose ample surface all these emotions chased each other, for yourself; it was beyond any description.

To aggravate it all, I did not show the smallest confusion at being thus caught en flagrant délit; I might be in the habit of being discovered daily in such misdemeanours for anything I evinced to the contrary. "I was so glad to see her" — in a languid tone "had a very bad headache and said I was not at home, but of course no such veto was for her" and then we kissed quite affectionately and I called Augustus who came in, and seeing the state of the case at once took forcible possession of the irate matron, while I finished my conversation with Lord Lansdowne, never even introducing him to her, though by doing so I should have been forgiven half my sins. When he was gone a comical struggle began between her and Augustus. She thought fit to try and sit him out, that she might give me her opinion of my conduct; but Augustus seeing her game, hadn't the smallest notion of being sat out in his own house; so they remained glaring at each other, to my intense amusement until seven-fifteen when she had to give it up, and decamp, children, nurses and perambulator, half an hour late for her dinner. "Insupportable old cat," Augustus exclaimed indignantly, watching the procession down the street, "we shan't have any more painting today . . . By the way, fair cousin mine, you have made an enemy, who, quite against his intention, has rendered you a celebrity."

"How?" "A certain young snob Francis Knolls [sic; see editor's note to follow] by name." "And who is Francis Knolls and what did I do to him?" "Don't you remember, a little dark man, bearing a strong family resemblance to the garçons of parisian restaurants who I introduced to you at Lady Pakenham's ball?" "Not in the least, but that doesn't matter, go on, what did I do to offend him?" "Answered with the pretty disdainful air habitual to you, when speaking to a person you don't admire, that you never danced square dances, when he asked you for a quadrille." "Oh, yes, I remember, and he went away in the rudest manner without answering; but it's a fact, I never do dance square dances, which I look upon as an invention of the righteous ones, to counteract the mischief done by valses." "Whatever your intentions may have been, you insulted Francis mortally: he told the story all over the room, meeting with very little sympathy, and wound up by complaining to the Prince of Wales, giving names and all. The Prince took the story up, laughed at Francis unmercifully, and never meets him now without quizzing him on the subject; of course, every one else follows HR Highness's example and the unhappy man will never hear the last of it. The Prince said to me only today 'I am dying to see this pretty disdainful cousin of yours, Augustus, who snubbed poor Francis so — you must introduce me at the Holfords' ball, only I'll take good care not to ask her for a square dance in case I might be snubbed too.' "

"Delicious! but Augustus, can you really manage the Holfords for us?" "Of course." "You duck. I do believe you are the sweetest most adorable man that ever existed!"

The men referred to in this long entry provide a hint as to Alice's fortunes in London. They are grand, but a touch rakish: great fun as flirts, but not likely to propose marriage.

Lord Carrington (1843–1928), the 3rd Baron, was a close friend of the Prince of Wales (later King Edward VII). He was acquainted with Nellie Clifden, one of the Prince's lady friends, and very much so with the French actress Hortense Schneider, and he got into scrapes both famous and infamous, although he was to become Lord Chamberlain. At King Edward's death, Carrington said, "He was the truest friend I ever had."

George William, 2nd Duke of Cambridge (1819–1904), the Prince of Wales's Uncle George, had the task of informing the Prince's future father-in-law of the Prince's early escapade with Nellie Clifden.

Alice's "Cocky", Henry Charles Keith Petty Fitz-Maurice, 5th Marquess of Lansdowne, was at this time a flighty twenty-three but was to become a very considerable public figure. He was to be – among other things – Lord of the Treasury, Under Secretary for War, Governor General of Canada, Viceroy of India and Foreign Secretary. Lansdowne House, one of the greatest private houses in London, was famous for its splendours. Lansdowne's country seat was Bowood Park, in Wiltshire, and he owned 140,000 acres in Britain and Ireland. It was level-headed of Alice to accept instantly and with equanimity that he was beyond her reach for anything more than a friendly flirtation.

Cornwallis West, grandson of the 2nd Earl Delaware, was born in 1835 and became a barrister of Lincoln's Inn in 1862. He was to be MP for Denbigh, and to develop Milford on Sea as a resort. He appears to have been the only man among those Alice met on this visit to London who invited her to meet the women in his family – his two sisters – and he was a more interesting man intellectually than her other admirers. Alice perceived this – and liked it until she found it, on closer acquaintance, rather hard to live up to. (Cornwallis West and his sisters disapproved of people who chattered while they were listening to music.)

"A certain young snob, Francis Knolls by name" may outwardly have resembled a French waiter, but Alice's pleasure in snubbing him makes her look rather silly. He was in fact Francis Knollys, son of General Sir William Knollys who was Comptroller and Treasurer to the Prince of Wales. Francis Knollys, four years older than the Prince, was appointed his private secretary in 1870 and survived in the post for forty-eight years, being, according to Giles St Aubyn in *Edward VII, Prince and King*, a wise, discreet, self-effacing, loyal and courageous man who showed unfailing fidelity and tact. He steered the Prince through all kinds of political and social problems and skilfully extricated

Mrs Miles, Mr Miles and Alice: pages from Alice's album decorated with her own paintings, all of which she dated 1874. The photographs may have been taken earlier.

Lady Miles after her husband came into his title, and her father-in-law Sir William Miles. Note the mistletoe – a touch of Alice's ironic humour, considering how much she disliked staying with him at Leigh Court (below).

him from a number of scandals. The word "snob", incidentally, had connotations slightly different from today's, meaning one who tried to push himself upwards in society rather than one who looked down upon others. It would not have applied to Francis Knollys.

Sunday 5th July

We spent the day at Maidenhead,[1] and Mother and I were the only ones that behaved with the slightest propriety, which accounts no doubt for our both being rather bored . . . Father, Mother and I took a most respectable and dull row, with Johnny Ogle as our sole companion. When I say that he (Mr Ogle) has few brains, no money, no position and no appearance, you will understand he did not do much towards enlivening us. Altogether I was not sorry to reach home at about eleven, my hands full of the water lilies I had rendered the gentlemen's lives a perfect burden to them, by making them carry. My only real amusement having lain in catching Cocky at the station, and just didn't he look ashamed of himself.

Monday 6th July

Captain Burnaby brought me my ticket for the "Blues" ball tonight. My vanity is content, but as far as the going is concerned, I am as far off as ever, seeing Mother has not the smallest chance of getting an invitation and she very properly will not let me go with May, or the Duchess of Montrose,[2] who have offered themselves as chaperones. We went to Mr West's house in the evening and there again my vanity was agreeably gratified by the immense breach of etiquette he committed in favour of my beaux yeux. Only fancy him passing over all the Duchesses and Marchionesses whose position entitled them to the honour, and picking me out of the whole room, to take down to supper, and others following just as they chose. Notwithstanding my anxiety about the "Blues" I found sufficient energy to be very much amused at the way they all glowered at me, and their spiteful remarks

---

[1] On the Thames — a popular resort for river parties, favoured by those bent on illicit dalliance.
[2] As will appear later, May Manners Sutton was not good chaperone material. Why the Duchess failed to make the grade I do not know.

were balm to my wounded spirit. A very nice fellow he is indeed, this Mr West; It appears he's ——'s cousin who, by the way, we met, and he told us Cornwallis had informed him, that the one thing in London worth seeing just at present was my hair. —— says he's worth about £500—1,000 a year and expectations, but unfortunately there's madness in the family, which is rather a drawback — still altogether I think he's worth cultivating, ne fut ce que pour l'amusement même.[1] Mother's invitation for the "Blues" never came, and I missed Aunt Aggie who could have taken me, and on going home I must plead guilty to crying myself to sleep with anger and vexation, not for the ball itself, but for my private reason for wanting to be there.[2]

Tuesday 7th July

A crowd of people called, Frank Gordon, young Vandeleur, Marquis Caumont de la Force, May, Capt. Burnaby, Edith Wood, Lansdowne, etc. The latter arrived just as Edith was going, and I am happy to say never had the civility even to shake hands with her, which was rather amusing, seeing the little monkey tried to make me believe he was rather in love with her.

That darling Augustus brought us the invitations to Mr Holford's[3] ball, we went at about 12, and I never saw anything so gorgeous as the room, the marble stair-case, and the whole effect of the tout ensemble. I am sorry to say the Prince of Wales was not there, as his stupid little wife chose to go and be confined yesterday[4]: but HRH was really the only thing wanting. The company was most select: I saw heaps more of the beautiful men, but as for the women, I must plead guilty to not perceiving anyone at all to be compared to Mother and myself, and I am happy to say the public (at any rate the male portion of it) was quite of the same opinion: the way we were run after, and admired and complimented, was something perfectly delightful, while the women were nearly expiring of envy, hatred, malice and all uncharitableness at being thus cut out, at the very end of the season. Before I had been five minutes in the room, one old

---

[1] ne fut ce que . . . if only for the fun of it.
[2] Presumably the chance of being introduced to the Prince of Wales.
[3] Probably these were the Holfords of Dorchester House, Park Lane.
[4] This baby was the Princess Victoria.

dowager[1] pointed me out to her friend remarking in a very unnecessarily loud tone "You see that lovely girl in white, with mauve
ribbons?" "Yes." "Well, that's Miss Miles, the Marquis of Lansdowne's fiancée." "Indeed!" and up went the old lady's eye glass, with
every appearance of interest — then after a critical survey "Well, the
young man has very good taste, she's the sweetest little face. What a
lucky girl to be sure!" Before the words were out of their mouth, Lord
Lansdowne, who had been elbowing his way up the room, came up to
me with as much empressement as if he hadn't seen me for months,
instead of having been sitting at 39 Eaton Place half the afternoon.
Both old ladies were delighted and watched us with the most lively
interest, more than ever persuaded of the truth of their prophecies.
Why, because people happen to be goodlooking, they should have
their names hacked about in this manner, is more than I can
understand, and too provoking. The only thing that consoles me is
somebody else having got up an opposition story, and spread a report
I refused him. I was certainly not over-gracious tonight, in fact we
quarrelled not a little, particularly about Mrs —— who is by no
means in the first class society, and of whom I remarked, with a
refinement of insolence only a woman can attain to, "You look as if
you were waiting for someone, Lord Lansdowne; surely you never
expected to see her here." He fired up, at this remark, just as I
intended he should, but I only laughed, saying with provoking
coolness, it was no sort of good losing his temper with me. Then after
fighting a little longer, we made it up again and he took me into
supper, sitting me down at the Royal Table, to make amends for his
bad behaviour.

> Alice then reports a conversation between a Captain Buckley
> and an anonymous Viscount, which must have been substantial-
> ly recounted to her by Augustus, who was probably a friend of
> both men. The Viscount, "happy heir to an earldom and
> somewhere about £80,000 a year", says to Buckley that he is
> thinking of marrying.

"Indeed, and have you fixed on the young lady, for if not I have one in
prospective [sic] for you who'd suit you down to the ground."

---

[1]Alice, at seventeen, would have seen anyone over thirty-five as fairly
ancient.

"Thanks, but there's a girl here tonight, out and out the best and newest thing in the room, who I think will do very well — come and I'll show her to you, then you shall find yours and we'll compare them", with which remark, his Lordship passed his hand through his friend's arm, and they proceeded to make a tour of discovery round the different ball-rooms. Both came to a stop at the same moment. "There's my beauty" exclaimed Capt. Buckley, pointing to me, then whirling round in all the entrain of a most delicious valse with Cornwallis West, the best dancer in the room. "And there's mine!" the viscount remarked indicating the same person "dancing with that goodlooking giant." (NB His Lordship is if anything an inch or two smaller than I am, and entertains the most profound and respectful admiration for everything over six foot.) "Why Ian [?] old fellow, I do believe we've hit on the same person" "Not a doubt of it" was the solemn answer "Isn't she perfect?" "I should rather think so, but who the devil can she be?" "A Miss Miles, Augustus Lumley's cousin, just arrived from Paris: I was introduced to her at Lady Pakenham's when she appeared for the first time." "My dear fellow," returned his friend "why couldn't you say so before, when I've been trying to find out all the evening who she is. Introduce me at once —" But that was more easily said than done; before they could approach me, Mr West had whirled me off into the middle of the dance again and afterwards we went to cool ourselves and do a little flirtation in the picture gallery, where Mr West picked out a beautiful Greuze, and informed me he was the artist who ought to have lived to paint me. It appears he [West] lives a few doors further down in Eaton Place, and has the most perfect painting room that ever was seen, and he wants me to come and sit there, declaring that we can have no decent light in the back drawing room, a statement in which Augustus is quite willing to aid and abet him. So I suppose I shall end in doing as they both want, indeed, I half promised to go tomorrow. Then he asked me to come and see him and his sisters next month in Wales, where they have a very beautiful place: That I think will be perfectly delightful and I may safely promise; as of course Mother will do as I wish her to — I think we can manage it on our return from Ireland — can? will, for I have made up my mind to go, and you know the proverb — ce que femme veut, Dieu le veut.[1]

Lord —— meanwhile had captured Augustus and they were

---

[1]ce que femme veut . . . : what woman wills, God wills.

hunting all over the rooms for me, without the smallest successs. "If I send her an invitation for my mother's ball on Thursday do you think she'll come?" the disappointed one asked in despair just before leaving. Augustus demurred, "I don't know, she's so awfully run after her time is generally pretty well filled up. Still send the invitation and I'll see what I can do for you." "Oh do! that's a good fellow" and with this assurance His Lordship departed, and Augustus, coming across me five minutes after he was out of sight, administered a lecture much in this wise — "Here have I been running after you for the last hour with Prince Teck in one hand, and —— in the other, both trying to be introduced, you nowhere to be found; and now you come sauntering up with Cornwallis just for all the world as if you'd done it on purpose." To which I answered "Augustus, dear old thing, don't be bad-tempered" and Cooke striking the first notes of his bewitching "Court Beauties" we were off before any further remonstrance could be addressed to us. We stayed till the very last, indeed I got hold of Mr Holford and made him tell the musicians to play just one more valse at the end of all things: it came at last to giving the same valse to four or five partners. Mr West went and waited downstairs to put me into the carriage but Lord Cole was beforehand with him and took that privilege on himself. What a delicious delicious evening it has been, I linger even in writing over the details of it. It was broad daylight long before we left, but drawing me into a window full in the radiance of the bright July sun, Mr West assured me I could stand the tell-tale unpitying light; and the glimpse I caught in a glass opposite, of a young unwearied face, with bright eyes dancing, and a faint flush on the normally too-white cheeks, made me fully agree with his decision. A neighbouring clock struck five, as our carriage rolled away, Father went to sleep in his corner, and Mother and I proceeded to compare notes of the evening we had equally enjoyed.

Wednesday 8th July

Got up somewhere between two and three, and despatched a couleur de rose missive to Mr West, to the effect that I was much too tired to keep my appointment, but that he might bring his painting materials over to us if he pleased. Upon receipt of which ten minutes afterwards he came himself to discuss our evening, minus the brushes. Sat to Augustus for the remainder of the day, and was very good, being too tired to talk and laugh and to move my head about in the way that drives him to despair, or do anything else except implicitly what I was told: a state of mind he very rarely finds me in. One interruption we had, Prince Camille de Polignac calling. I forget whether I said I met him last night, and as Mother thought fit not to cut him gave him a valse, as he came to my assistance when that rude girl seized Lord Lansdowne intimating it was her dance, and she should not let him off it: what a difference he must see between my behaviour to him and the saucy remarks I gratify him with, and that of all those grasping young young husband hunters. Prince Camille, who has plenty of sense when he thinks fit to use it, duly appreciated the effect we were creating, and will of course retail it to Edmond with some fabulous stories of the young handsome millionaires I have at my feet, that I took care to regale him with. After five minutes tête à tête, I made him come into the painting room, which not appreciating as he ought to, he took his departure just as I intended. I have no sort of idea of encouraging any of the family.

* * * * *

We dined with the Somersets and I submitted to listen to my aunt's strictures on my conduct, with every appearance of contrition, which considering Prince Camille's recent visit, must be looked upon as slightly hypocritical. However I am restored to favour which is all that's required. Aggie[1] was at the ball too last night, and considering she has had the whole season here, I think she ought to be perfectly ashamed of herself, for she'd scarcely any partners, most of them boys, and does not number in the list one single elder son. I introduced Lord Hinchingbrooke[2] to her but he never asked her to dance, and would have introduced Lansdowne, only he remarked with more naïveté than politeness "Please don't, she's not goodlooking enough, and I must say I like my partners to be very pretty and − amiable!" This last being a side thrust at me, as we were in the midst of our little quarrel. But though her appearance is not calculated to set men at variance, little Aggie is not half a bad girl. I gave her a most amusing description of the manner in which her mother had caught me: and though she struggled against it, the absurdity of my recital got the better of her conscientious scruples, and she couldn't help laughing. Altogether we passed a sufficiently pleasant evening.

[1]Her cousin and friend, Aunt Agatha's daughter.
[2]Heir to the Earl of Sandwich.

Thursday 9th July

Capt. Campbell sent us a card for the Guards' party, but look about as well as I could, not a sign could I see of him. I was rather angry till Augustus began lecturing me, as he thinks his position of chaperone entitles him to. "Oh les femmes! les femmes! and the prettier they are the more unreasonable they become. Instead of being duly grateful to poor Beauty for not forgetting to send you your card in the midst of such trouble, you are working yourself up into quite a rage with him, to be paid with interest on the very next opportunity, for not dancing attendance on you, when he got a telegram yesterday from the north of Scotland, calling him to his father's death-bed." "That alters the question, of course: but you must own it is very annoying of his father to go and die, just when I required his services, besides he —" "Alice!" Mother exclaimed, touching my arm, "stop fighting with Augustus for a moment and give us your attention." And turning round I became conscious of the presence of Capt. Buckley and a small goodlooking man with the brightest and frankest of blue eyes, curly dark hair, a fair beard, and a large well-formed mouth showing the whitest rows of even teeth, who was introduced to me as Lord ——[1]. I was greatly taken with the bright open face, and I believe if we had both followed our natural instinct, we would have shaken hands on the spot: but such a breach of decorum was not to be dreamt of in the middle of London and the enlightened 19th century, so I bowed as graciously as I could, and he uncovered his curly head in a ceremonious salute, and after making us promise to go that night to his Father's ball and securing a valse for himself, went on with his friend Ian [?] Buckley, who it appears has taken an immense fancy to me, which I am very glad of, as he may one of these days be very useful indeed. Walked about a little with the Marquis Caumont de la Force, but soon tired of that amusement: besides it's entirely against my principles wasting my time with a french-man when it is possible to employ it otherwise.

* * * * *

Found a magnificent five guinea bouquet all delicate basket-work, white satin ribbon, lace and hothouse flowers on our return home. There is no doubt but that it was for Mother from the doting Poodle,[2]

---

[1]Clearly this was the Viscount who, with his friend Buckley, had been in pursuit of Alice at the Holfords' ball.
[2]Unidentified. I suspect there was more than one.

but still as I took possession of it, and told everyone it was mine, it didn't much signify. Mother went off directly after dinner to take May, with whom she was to go to the opera, but that foolish virgin had been having one of the stand-up fights, she every now and then treats her lord and master to, about Mrs Villebois and her ball I believe, and had been crying and screeching in the most orthodox hysterics, until she had rendered herself perfectly unfit to be seen for the next twelve hours at least; so Mother came rushing back to me, routed me off the sofa where I had composed myself for a refreshing slumber, and dressed me so quickly, that we really got there in very decent time. I have a kind of vague idea that "Romeo and Juliet" was the name of the opera, and that Patti and Mario sang but Frank Gordon and later Lord Cole, chattered to me too incessantly for my remembrance of the piece to be anything but confused. It appears that Mr Gordon is "Baby" Stewart's predecessor, and some people are naughty enough to say even occasional successor up to the present time: certain it is, he came to meet May tonight, and I think deserves great praise for the stoic manner in which he concealed his pain at the queen of his affections not being forthcoming. Herbert Wilson was in the pit staring at us, as if he'd never seen a pretty woman before. Happily he didn't recognise us, indeed I at least defied recognition, seeing the last time we met, I was five and a half and one of the most insupportable specimens to be found, even of that insupportable age. We left a little before the end, as we had to go home and dress: but even then, hurry as much as we could, we didn't reach the ball much before two, and I am sorry to say I was by no means looking my best, being so dead tired that not withstanding having fortified myself with chicken and champagne, I nearly broke down in the dreadfully energetic valse Lord —— insisted on my taking and was most thankful when he went and fetched one of his mother's shawls, and took me to sit in the garden.

* * * * *

A most horribly energetic young man is Monsieur le Vicomte, I mastered that much of his character tonight. Forever hunting, shooting, jumping, rowing, gymnastic-ing, and a whole host more of those insupportable accomplishments: valses as if his salvation depended on not losing one note of the music, and enjoys it thoroughly all the while: so I suppose I must look upon his sitting out two dances for which he was engaged, quietly with me, as a great victory over these unpleasant instincts . . .

> The "Romeo and Juliet" chattered through by Alice and her
> friends would have been *Roméo et Juliette* by Gounod
> (1818—1893), at the Royal Opera House, Covent Garden (rebuilt
> in 1858), with Adelina Patti and Giovanni Mario in the leading
> roles. The cavalier attitude of fashionable society to cultural
> events could hardly be better illustrated than by the Miles party's
> behaviour: arriving late, leaving before the end and talking
> throughout. Some twenty years later George Bernard Shaw,
> writing as a music critic, was still complaining of such be-
> haviour. "How they talked! One young lady, who must, I should
> think, be the champion chatterbox of the universe, so outdid
> with her tongue [the performer] that I stole three times through
> the east gallery merely to see whether she had stopped from
> exhaustion: but she was as fresh as an aviary each time."[1]

Saturday 11th July

As both Augustus and Mr West have been worrying me to ever since
the Holfords' today I went to luncheon at the latter, and sat to them
afterwards. I was introduced to Miss Nina and Florence West, very
nice and rather goodlooking girls both of them. What a jolly time of it
they must have to be sure, leading this bachelor life with their
brother, who is perfectly devoted to them, and would no more dream
of contradicting them than he would dream of contradicting me —
They have a most beautiful house, and his painting room is a perfect
bijou, situated away from the other apartments, and with a public
and private entrée, all quite correct. I should not the least mind sitting
to Mr West, for instead of scolding me every time I move, as Augustus
does and occasionally informing me I'm "a little [two indecipherable
French words]" which though perhaps true, is not pleasant to one's
feelings to be perpetually reminded of — he praised me as much as my
hard-hearted cousin abuses me, let me move whenever I felt inclined,
and had the most delicious little repast for me at five thirty composed
of genuine french coffee, strawberries and cream, peaches, grapes,
cakes, and all sorts of other little delicacies: still truth forces me to
confess that though he looked at me quite as intently as does
Augustus, somehow or other his sketch didn't seem to advance.

* * * * *

[1]*GBS on Music*, Pelican, 1962.

Imagine my disgust when I got home to find that Lansdowne and Lord —— had both called. The former I don't care about, having been just as well employed as in talking to him, but I am most annoyed at missing the latter. Why on earth couldn't the stupid fellow tell me last night that he meant to come.

Sunday 12th July

Went and lunched with May, having got up too late for church, then paid a solemn visit to the Somersets, walked about a little with Aggie in the Square, discussing Wells[1] memories, and bemoaning over the season that will be so soon past; and then went home as our relatives, having done morning and afternoon, announced their intention of setting off for evening church. Jane Burton dined with me, and after dinner Edith Wood arrived to pay me a visit, and kept us in fits of laughing till ten thirty. There is not a naughty story or fie-fie anecdote making the tour of London, that that girl is not perfectly acquainted with: and the spiciest history of all her spicy repertoire does not lose the slightest particle of flavour in her way of telling it: a more amusing companion it would be difficult to find.

Tonight we were regaled with all Schneider's latest misdeeds, how the Duke of Cambridge favoured the Blues with a most à propos visit and was with difficulty kept from entering Lord Carrington's room, where he would have found the fair comedienne: as it was she remained there all day, as the Duke, suspecting some such mischief was going on, [stayed] lounging about the barracks half the afternoon. Charlie Carrington too had to join him, as he could not pretend he was in his bath all day, so Mlle Schneider had plenty of leisure to reflect on her misdeeds in this enforced solitude and quietness. Then before we had recovered from that story, Edith had us in convulsions again, recounting how a certain Charlie —— [?] took it on himself to box Capt. Burnaby's ears, for barricading him up in his room with a certain fair lady who was there strictly against the rules. On receiving the fully merited soufflet, Henan turned in a fury, Capt. —— [?] took to his heels, the other gave chase, and for half an hour they careered

[1]Perhaps Aggie and Alice had been to school together at Wells. I have been able to find no explanation of these "memories", so have to guess.

after each other round the barrack square to the intense amusement of
the other officers: both — this is the most ludicrous part of the whole
thing — being bare-footed and in their night gowns; the dispute
having taken place at night.

It is to be supposed that the night air penetrating their scanty
garments cooled their ardour, for certain it is they finished by shaking
hands, instead of calling each other out with murderous intentions.
Having digested this history we proceeded to pick May to pieces a
little in her turn: and pass the long defile of her — her — fancies shall
we call them? in review: then we went on to her family: it appears her
mother was a cocotte's illegitimate daughter and I really think that if
from the abode of bliss where the old lady is receiving the reward of
the virtues she practised so persistently on earth, she could look down
on Belgravia 1868, she would have no sort of reason to complain of
her fair descendant's too strict ideas and rigid interpretation of the 7th
commandment. Having settled that point to our satisfaction we went
on to Edith's particular friend Mrs Du Cane, one of Capt. Armitage's
former loves, honourably mentioned in the following verses that when
they were written made the tour of every club in London.

Les voici:

> A was Armitage so gallant and bold
> B is the Buckley: her story's soon told
> C stands for Copley he brought her to shame
> D is the donkey who made her Du Cane

* * * * *

a pleasant thing to be shown up in this manner, n'est ce pas? At
ten-thirty Edith departed after nearly extinguishing us with laughter,
I must say I rather like her in spite of Augustus, qui se trouve mal[1], at
the mere mention of her name, firstly from instinctive aversion and
secondly from the spiteful story he heard her tell about his admiration
for my hair and the manner in which we spend the time supposed to
be dedicated to the advancement of my picture. It was nasty of her
certainly but one must pay for everything in this world, most of all for
one's amusements.

* * * * *

[1]qui se trouve mal — who feels sick.

The "Schneider" imprisoned in Lord Carrington's room was Hortense Schneider, singer and *comédienne*, who reigned supreme as "the true queen" of Paris during the 1860s. On arriving at the gate reserved for royalty at the Paris Exhibition, she announced that she was "la Grande Duchesse de Gérolstein" — this being the title of the operetta in which she was currently starring. It was alleged that the Prince of Wales neglected his pregnant wife in Schneider's favour.

Tuesday 14th July

Five thirty a.m. Well, I am back again and having slipped on my comfortable nightgown and robe de chambre, let down my hair, and taken every other disposition for ease, I feel myself still, notwithstanding the hour, so totally incapable of going to sleep that I draw up a low chair to the writing table, and return to you, my little silent confidant.

* * * * *

It has been a delicious evening — delicious! — Full stop. I push back a tiresome mass of hair, out of my eyes: take a turn round the room, look out of the window at this busy London waking already; returning to active life before I have even closed my eyes; then come back to you my book again and try and recall the details of Mrs Holford's ball.

The beginning was not promising, he was not there, and though I had tried to persuade him he oughtn't to come, woman-like I was quite furious at being so well obeyed, and I flirted tremendously with the Marquis Caumont de la Force in consequence, at least so Mother told me, I must say I have no plain remembrance of it; but Caumont left one-thirty, and still no signs of the truant, so I turned my attention to Sir Samuel Hayes, who being unable of course to appreciate my motives, was greatly flattered. I remember we settled ourselves at one corner of the supper table and talked and laughed immensely: Anyone to have watched us, his empressé face and manner, my sparkling restless eyes, bright smiles and merry constant laugh would have said "How those two are enjoying themselves!" — So much for appearances: truly — as the gentleman once remarked to a maiden lady of eight-and-thirty, who informed him she was just twenty-five — you should not trust in them, for they are occasionally most deceptive. Augustus meanwhile was watching my proceedings with evident disapproval, but I was getting desperate and didn't care in the least:

the more he frowned the brighter I looked. At last, just as I was extracting a little amusement out of Sir Sammy, by reminding him of his daring leap after Lady Diana Beauclerc's glove, and some other little passages in his history he deemed me in perfect ignorance of, Augustus lost patience and whispered as he bent over my shoulder, apparently to recommend some particularly fine grapes — "Your friend of the broken arm[1] is upstairs — when you are quite tired of talking to this Guardsman" and then vanished, leaving me to make what use of the information I pleased.

Darling boy! I'm sure no one ever had such a cousin as him! — What regular relation supposing him and a very unlikely supposition it is — to be equally[2] would ever behave with half the tact and esprit — As soon as he was out of sight my conduct underwent a sudden change. "Sir Samuel" I said, pushing away the grapes he had given me, "I can't possibly eat any more, and that valse I hear in the distance is perfectly bewitching. Let's go upstairs." To which he answered "Miss Miles, your will is law. But" — with a sidelong glance at my head "Even admitting your ears to be as quick of hearing as they are fair to look upon, excuse me for doubting your capability of catching the faintest strains of music at this distance. Why not say truthfully you are tired of this room and of my society, and therefore you wish to go upstairs."

— I suppressed the faintest soupçon of a yawn; his arguing the point bored me. — "It's quite possible but surely you should not find fault with me, for sparing your vanity the confession. — Sir Samuel, now I come to think of it, we're both talking great nonsense and the sooner we go back to the ballroom the better." So there was nothing for him to do after this, but to offer me his arm and back we went. My valse, invented as a plausible pretext on the spot, turned out to be no fiction: valsing they were. We took a turn too, as the best means for my showing myself and when we stopped the first person who came up to me to ask for the next, was Lord ——

* * * * *

"I thought you never were coming" I said reproachfully as we took our places. "I suppose I ought not to have, as it is I got up to do it." "Poor fellow" very compassionately "How is your arm" "Making me feel it

[1]The mysterious Viscount had dislocated his shoulder at gymnastics.
[2]"equally concerned"? "equally kind"? Alice has left something out — but it was 5a.m.!

rather more than is pleasant: do you mind trying to dance with the left arm." "Not in the least" and we carried out the suggestion to the great amazement of the rest of the room who thought it was done for effect and the utter horror of little Francis Knolls, watching me with a Mephistoles [*sic*] cast of countenance from a doorway opposite.

*   *   *   *   *

Edith Wood is here tonight, a regular little rose bud in the midst of all her pink drapery and looking perfectly bewitching. It appears that while I was engaged with Sir Samuel downstairs, one of her partners had gone up and spoken to Lord Petersham. When he came back again Edith asked "Who was that you were talking to?" "Petersham: don't you know him?" "No, but I particularly wish to, do go and get him and introduce him to me" which was accordingly done. Seeing me nowhere he asked her for a valse which she promised, but fate and I had ordained she should have no chance that night of redeeming her word.

> So the mystery man is identified. Alice continues to delete his name, but once known it can usually be made out, and hereafter I use it whenever the identification is certain. Petersham was born on January 9th 1844 and was educated at Queen's College, Belfast, and Christ Church College, Oxford. The earldom to which he was the "happy heir" was that of Harrington to which he succeeded in 1881. He became the owner of 13,000 acres, with seats at Elveston Castle, Derby, and Gawsforth, Macclesfield.

When our dance was over we had gone into the supper room where we still were when they began to play the next valse. "Botheration" he exclaimed impatiently, "Shall we be obliged to go upstairs?" "Not if you would sooner stay here: I am too tired to dance this or indeed more at all until it is absolutely necessary." Turning to my partner a stupid young diplomat who didn't know when he was de trop and now came up triumphantly to claim me "I am very sorry, but you see I am at supper, and we are going directly afterwards." "Well, that was neatly done" Lord Petersham exclaimed as soon as he was out of hearing. "Aren't you engaged?" I asked. "Oh dear me yes, but gentlemen have the advantage that their partners can't run up and claim them just at the precise moment when they are least wanted, like we are constantly doing." I might have contradicted him, remembering the enterprising young lady who pounced so inopportunely on Lord Lansdowne at the Holfords' only I didn't and we soon passed to more interesting subjects, until the band striking up "Pauline" that most irresistible of all Cooke's irresistible valses, neither of us, not even my poor wounded friend, whose arm was paining him a good deal, could withstand going and taking a turn. "That's the girl I ought to have danced the last thing with" he whispered as we left the supper-room "Standing opposite there in pink": it was my fair friend Edith, wrapped in her opera cloak, flirting more than considerably with Francis Knolls. I could not resist the temptation of amazing her and cutting him, so brought astonished Lord Petersham to a full stop before her. "Hasn't it been a delicious ball, Edith?" I asked utterly ignoring Mr Knolls' very existence. She took us both in, I standing with my hand lying on Petersham's arm, and uttered a very doubtful "Yes". "I see you are going" I continued sublimely unconscious of anything wrong. "Goodnight dear" and stooping forward I kissed her, quite affectionately and then we moved on, reaching the ball-room, to find it quite deserted, save by two or three adventurous couples, and the bewitching music still in full strain. –

Oh the divine valse we had, quicker, faster, not waiting for a moment's breath, but on, on, until the room spun round, everything seemed unreal, and we felt nothing but the melody till at last imperceptibly the music died away and I found myself, when I could look clearly round me again, alone with him in the Conservatory. The playing of a small fountain, the only sound that broke the stillness. I went and leant my head under it, feeling almost faint, the cold water revived me and I came back to the sofa, the crystal drops sparkling on my hair and forehead, and nestling like dew in the heart of the rose he had given me but which was dropping its petals now – He looked at me admiringly – "Lovely!" then there was a silence broken by his saying with a sigh "What a delicious Valse" – "Yes, yet do you know I have the reputation of not liking dancing." "It is a heresy I should never have dreamt of accusing you of": "And yet it is true – to a certain extent. I know it is an old-fashioned idea but I hate dancing with everyone and from some men I have an absolutely physical shrinking" " Which I perfectly understand" – a short silence again: then in a much lower tone "I hope you never experienced anything of the sort, when dancing with me?" "No!" –

He scarcely could have heard the word but saw what it was by the movement of the lips, and we were silent again, only broken by mother's entrance two minutes afterwards.

"My dear child!" she exclaimed "Are you aware that everyone is going, not a soul left in the ball-room, the musicians decamped, and last but not least, its nearly five o'clock and I am dead tired. Do come." Which I did, though a little unwillingly; he put me into the carriage and then turned to walk home with Capt. Buckley. — So we both came home, very well content with our evening and now — well just now, it is striking from that dainty little Sèvres clock, that records the flight of time on its rose-crowned dial, six o'clock: which means that I have been gossiping exactly an hour with you, my book, and had better lock you up, and excluding the bright daylight and busy noises of the street, compose myself to sleep for the next five hours at least.

> Alice preferred the waltz to more old-fashioned dances, as we know from her refusal to dance a quadrille with Francis Knollys. The waltz had been danced in Vienna as early as 1773, but had remained almost "universally opposed as improper" for half a century. In 1805 Dr Burney called it a "riotous German dance of modern invention" — though it was based on an old form of peasant dance. He went on: "The verb *waltzen* . . . implies to roll, wallow . . . roll in the dirt. What analogy there may be between these acceptations and the dance, we pretend not to say; but having seen it performed by a select party of foreigners, we could not help reflecting how uneasy an English mother would be to see her daughter so familiarly treated, and still more to witness the obliging manner in which the freedom is returned by the females." Even in the second half of the nineteenth century a sermon was preached asking if parents would allow their daughters to submit to such intimate bodily contact with young men anywhere except in the ballroom. Whether or not the unwonted intimacy of the dance made Alice shrink when a partner was not to her taste, she was well aware of how charming men found a fastidious daintiness, and used this to good effect on other occasions.

Tuesday 14th July

Had a regular domestic Row; — not to be inscribed here however, as it was no particular business of mine and I had, I am happy to say, no personal concern in it.

The London Season, 1868

Thursday 16th July

The first really wretched day that I have indulged in since I have been in London. Capt. Buckley, who is kind enough to take a most lively interest in my proceedings, promised Mother to get up a picnic for Friday, and here we are the very day before and have never heard a word from him. Add to this that it was tremendously hot, and I felt utterly listless and out of sorts at the idea of being marched off to Ireland Sunday, for Father swears that not a day longer will he stop: this combination of afflictions was too much for me, and I cried for half an hour from sheer despair and weariness, and would have continued much longer, only Father insisted on me going with him to lunch at May's, which, at that particular time, and in my present frame of mind, was more than all things utterly distasteful to me. However I got through it somehow or other, talked to Kit D[1], snubbed an odious old Col., then pleading a bad headache went home. Still no news of Mr Buckley. At last as necessity is the mother of invention, I hit on the bright idea of despatching a note to Lord Petersham to know if he could enlighten us as to what we were to do: here is his answer: "Dear Mrs Miles" (I always write in D's[2] name in the most prudent manner) "Dear Mrs Miles — I don't know anything about anything, so can't give you any orders, as you call them. I am engaged for dinner tomorrow night, but that is my only engagement, so shall come to luncheon at your house, if I may, and we can arrange something amusing for ourselves, in spite of Buckley's desertion. Yours very truly,
Petersham.
I intended to have seen you today, but had such a bad sore throat that I stayed indoors."

* * * * *

I cheered up again on the receipt of this letter; and examined myself minutely in a large mirror to see if this morning's tears, that I might have spared myself after all, had materially damaged my appearance. No! It's rather a white little face that looks back at me, and the lines under the eyes, always dark, are darker than usual, but these are mere trifles a good night's rest will perfectly remove — and I need not

[1]Probably Mr Denison, who reappears later.
[2]D——: Alice's mother. What the nickname was I have not discovered.

torment myself about my appearance not being fully equal to the emergency.

> Evidently a good deal happened on Friday, July 17th, for Alice filled no less than eighteen sides of her notebook, but cut most of it out. By the 18th she was preparing reluctantly to leave London and was in some kind of nervous state, relating perhaps to the domestic "row", the heat, and her attack of weeping.

Saturday 18th July

My last day in London, and a sufficiently gloomy one too, seeing I was so much worse that they sent for the Dr who came to see me twice; shook his head, talked about over-excitement, gave me some very nasty medicine and departed. I slept all day and on waking at about five-thirty after his last visit sent for Louisa to know what had occurred. She brought me Lord Lansdowne's and Capt. Buckley's cards, and I roused myself sufficiently to be very amused by the curious coincidence of their calling together — for of course, after mother's remarks,[1] the latter thought he was brought to do gooseberry, and never attached a word of belief to Louisa's statement that Miss Miles was in, but not well enough to receive his Lordship. Then there was a very nice note from Mr West, sending me some photographs and a most cordial invitation to Ruthin, his place in Wales: finally the following scrawl from Aggie. "Dearest Ally — We came to see you but found you asleep so left you so" (only fancy if I'd been receiving Capt. B and Lord Lansdowne instead of being thus innocently employed — I declare they would have caught me again!). "I am very very sorry to hear you are going tomorrow and expect Lord Petersham will be in the depths of despair. I'll try and come and see you tomorrow after morning church, till then goodbye, ever thine, AGS."

---

[1]"Mother's remarks" refer to a passage so obscure and so much defaced that I have omitted it. It concerns a conversation between Mrs Miles and Captain Buckley, after the Holfords' ball.

Summer Visiting

HE Season shaded off into country visiting for most of its participants; and for the Miles family — because Alice's father had as yet no house in England — such visits were essential if they were not to beat a retreat to France, which Alice would certainly deplore. Their first call was to Limerick in Ireland, to relations of Mrs Miles. The change from recent weeks was extreme.

Sunday 2nd August, 1868

I write from Carass, Ireland, where we have been a long time now[1] — vegetating — for life this calm and uneventful existence can hardly be

[1]Only about ten days, in fact.

termed. Sunday night, the 19th July was I taken away from the dear old house 39 Eaton Place, dear to me in the short space of time from all its pleasant memories. I was miserable at leaving it and utterly unfit to travel; add to all this that I cried from sheer disgust during half the journey, and you will have a faint idea of the object I was when I arrived. − I don't know that I am particularly unhappy here now once I've settled down; − though Heaven knows there's not an earthly thing to do, or read, or even speculate on; but I am so thoroughly tired out, that the rest is rather refreshing physically and mentally. I do no earthly thing but eat, sleep, drink an inordinate amount of milk and cream, and lay [sic] under the green trees with my half-closed, speculating vaguely on the future, through all the long hot summer days. After the excitement and wear and tear of London, there is a certain relief in the consciousness that you may look as white and pale, and be as tired as you please, without anyone remarking on it; and indulge in low spirits without any fear of a sudden ring warning you to smile and put on your company manners again, as gracefully as may be.

* * * * *

There have been great changes since I was here last, as my Uncle David has thought fit to take himself a wife in the shape of the honourable Isabella Massey, Lord Clarina's youngest daughter; a maiden of twenty-eight, very plain, totally devoid of manner, intensely amiable; in fact in every way as great a nonentity as you could reasonably have expected even him to have selected.

The best thing about her to my mind, are her brothers, and they are charming: the third, Lionel, a Colonel in the Scots Fusiliers, particularly so. Fancy meeting a really goodlooking Guardsman, up here in the wilds! Miracles, or "Miwacles" as my friend the very rev. bishop of Gibraltar pronounces it, will never cease. Then there is Hugh, the second, a stalwart young farmer, très bon camarade[1], and more goodnatured than it is possible to say. In fact Carass might be made habitable enough if only Isabel would have the penetration to invite her brothers: but she hasn't the faintest idea of doing anything of the sort. They come occasionally and dine and spend the night, leaving next morning − nothing more!

A certain Miss Mary Massey, a cousin of Isabel's, is the only person

---

[1]très bon camarade − very "good pal".

staying here: a good honest sort of girl of twenty two, with all the fresh naïve ideas naturally induced by a life-long sojourn amongst the Irish mountains. It is curious to see how this sort of people, brought up in this state of civilised uncivilisation, believe in woman's virtue, man's honour, conjugal felicity, disinterested affection; and all those other high-sounding names, that to us living in the midst of a corrupt world, are names and names only. I had been expatiating in no measured terms, on the imbecility of a girl who, entirely penniless herself, had through some romantic nonsense refused the heir to a peerage and fabulous wealth; a very charming young man too, into the bargain; I shall never forget the surprised tone in which Mary answered "But my dear, of course she couldn't marry him, if she didn't love him" and then she added with great emphasis, as if that quite settled the point "It wouldn't have been doing her duty." "I can't say I agree with you," I answered, drawing for some more of those delightfully fresh remarks that have all the charm of novelty to me "I consider it every girl's duty to marry £80,000 a year, if a beneficent Providence vouchsafes her the opportunity: and more particularly so, when Pluto arrives as in the present case, disguised as a goodlooking young nobleman. Why, the girl must have refused him in a fit of temporary insanity and probably has had full time to regret it since. And not withstanding your fine notions, Mary, let me tell you if I was a young marquis with £50,000 a year I'd be very sorry to propose to you, if I didn't mean to be accepted, even if I was not a downright Apollo. Love in a cottage overgrown with roses is a very fine thing in theory, but depend upon it, love in a palace is the pleasanter of the two; as, in real life, when the first few enchanting weeks are over, you are apt to be tormented by invasions of earwigs out of the heart of your favourite creeper, and remarks more practical than pleasant from your husband if the cookery and comfort of the rose-embowered establishment does not quite come up to the ideal he had formed. Love is a charming thing in itself and gives undoubtedly a delicate flavour to life, not to be imparted by anything else, but as in a cunningly-wrought sauce, you must have all the other ingredients as well. Otherwise it will be an utter failure. Do you understand?" "Yes, but I think all that depends greatly on the manner in which you have been brought up. I should be supremely happy as the wife of a poor curate I was attached to: in fact a crowd of useless luxuries would only embarrass me; while you, do you think, Alice, you could exist without them?"

"I should be very sorry to try. Beauty, music, bright colours, odours, flowers, are as necessary to me as the very air I breathe, and what life would be without them I decline even to contemplate. As a gentleman I had succeeded in irritating pretty considerably once informed me, I am like one of those 'white, waxen-looking exotica, nurtured in a hot-house, conveyed into a drawing room with the greatest care, and who so long as they are only asked to look beautiful and diffuse a delicious perfume, fulfil their duty to perfection. But as for expecting devotion, self-sacrifice and those other virtues so beautiful in woman' (continued my irate admirer) 'from one of these spoilt children of nature, you might as well, to take a Bible illustration, expect of thistles to gather grapes. No! these women, angels in prosperity, desert you at the first breath of adversity: or if forced to stay and encounter it, droop their delicate heads and die. Carriages and opera boxes, velvet point lace and diamonds, are objects of necessity to them, and combined form a paradise from which no rash act of their own, such as an ill-assorted marriage, or romantic affection, will ever expel them.'

"So said my angry friend, Mary, and I assure you on such subjects his authority is held to be unexceptionable; so you must pity instead of blaming me, for to this class of women, he declared, I belong." "Then he told an audacious lie, and ought to be ashamed of himself" and Mary flamed up with pretty indignation, in defence of her friend who would not defend herself. "As for you Alice, you calumniate yourself in talking like that, for I am sure if you were really tried, you would be capable of any sacrifice in behalf of one you were really fond of." "Perhaps so!" and I sighed a little wearily, knowing well as I do what infinite depths of tenderness I hide under the cynical and indifferent composure habitual to me, and wondering if to me will ever come that spark of divine flame, that would perforce call it all to light.

* * * * *

Col. Massey arrived shortly after this conversation, and according to my wont I was as amiable to him, as if I had never been led into such a bitter denunciation of all detrimentals.[1] Mary watched me with wondering eyes for the first half hour, then gave me up as incomprehensible, which perhaps under the circumstances was about the wisest

---

[1] Current slang for charming men who happened to be undesirable as husbands because they lacked either money or seriousness. Often used of portionless younger sons.

thing she could do. Lionel proposed to teach me croquet: now for croquet in the abstract I entertain a most profound contempt, looking upon it as a stupid invention to conduce to flirting, that is wholly beneath the notice of an adept in the art. Still it may be useful in individual cases, besides Mary adores it, so though neither the Guardsman or myself knew the first rudiments of the game, and both entertained a strong predilection for cheating when it could be done with impunity — I put on my neatest pair of boots and we knocked about the balls, greatly to our own satisfaction, and the other players' unqualified disapproval. When we had at last by dint of continual cheating and every other evil device succeeded in convincing Mary of our total incapacity, she consented to release us.

> Alice proceeded, predictably, to flirt with Lionel against a beautiful and romantic background. While walking (un-chaperoned) they came upon a poor Irish cabin in which burned a peat fire. Alice, always willing to dispose herself to the most picturesque advantage, took possession at once.

We entered straightaway, and five minutes later formed as charming a little domestic group, as ever painter transferred to canvas: I on the sole chair the cabin boasted of; drawn close into the bright fire of turf and burning logs: the prettiest of kittens perfectly at home on my lap, and making playful jumps at my watch chain, I held tantalisingly above its head: Lionel looking down on us from his six foot two, not, I am sorry to say with the contempt we merited, but with hearty appreciation of the fun: indeed he got a scratch from Pussy later, for trying to join in the game. Only fancy if Isabel in a fit of benevolence had chosen to visit that especial cottage! how she would have stared at finding her favourite brother and scapegrace niece so perfectly at home instead of the poverty she intended to relieve: or supposing again our various partners could have seen us — in this poor Irish cabin; and heard our merry laughter over a kitten's tricks. The spoilt London beauty and the aristocratic blasé young Guardsman behaving for all the world like two children just escaped from school. Happily, however, no one did see us, so there was nothing to prevent our enjoying ourselves, and being to the full as undignified as we pleased.

*   *   *   *   *

I spent Saturday, Sunday and part of Monday at Ballinoe, with my cousins the Coxes, and very pleasant days they were. It was all so totally new, I could not help being amused, but as a continuance I am not prepared to say I should at all like this primitif mode of living. I am fonder of my little soldier cousin Willie than I am of most people; he was there and no dog could have been more devoted to me. So we used to take long walks, wander about among the gooseberries and currants in the old-fashioned kitchen garden discussing philosophical rubbish, or else he recounting his adventures en amour for my instruction and amusement. Sunday we rode to the church ten miles distant, and allowed ourselves ample time for arriving, supposing we cantered. But the day was oppressively hot and I had no idea of running the risk of a sun-stroke, besides it is difficult to talk when you are in rapid motion, so it ended in our walking the whole way; and as children say "the consequence was" we arrived rather late: and our apparition, me in Wolverhausen habit, bouquet, veil reaching to the nose, etc., as complete a get-up as if I was going to Rotten Row, with Willie in his military undress and jingling spurs, created rather a diversion, walking down the aisle of the little country church, just as the congregation were beginning to get tired of a prosey sermon. Altogether I enjoyed myself very much with my cousins, and my stay at Ballinoe is amongst my pleasantest souvenirs of Ireland. Wednesday the 6th we leave; and I must say without the slightest sorrow on my part, my only regret being that we didn't go before: as by this arrangement we have only three days at Mr West's, for whose château we are now bound.

So the narrative of Alice's visit to Ireland concludes. The unthinking way in which Alice invaded a cottage, as though it existed simply as a piece of "scenery" to set her off, rather than as someone's home, underlines the gulf between a "big house" and its tenantry as much as it does her own selfishness.

Next stop was Ruthin Castle, which was then the home of Cornwallis West. It was a creation of the nineteenth century, the earliest part built within the ruined walls of a medieval castle, at the head of the Vale of Clwyd in North Wales. Ten thousand acres went with it, and also Milford on Sea in Hampshire.

Ruthin Castle, Saturday night, 8th August.

I sit down to transmit to paper my ideas concerning our present residence and must begin by owning I am at once delighted and disappointed. Ruthin itself — and this is what pleases me — is a perfect palace and situated in the midst of scenery that would transport a poet or painter; but I being neither the one nor the other, look prosaically to the amount of golden sovereigns these beauteous acres would produce; and the sum total, according to the lowest calculation, is by no means despicable. Unhappily all this is the property of the invalided elder brother; but Cornwallis is certain to inherit it at his death, as well as Newlands, a beautiful place in the south of England from his mother; so he is by no means so bad a parti as his cousin declared, and I was right in my conjectures of his being perfectly worth cultivating in every way. All this contents me much; now for my disappointment. Instead of the charming party I expected to meet, picked from all that London holds most select, we have fallen, Mother and I, two pretty unsympathising mondaines, into the midst of the arts, represented by individuals famous for their knowledge of painting, dirty bits of metal, precious stones in the rough, and such other treasures; talented doubtless as is proved by their discrimination in such matters; but otherwise singularly uninteresting. Now I delight in a good picture when I see it, and proportionally abominate the wretched daubs modern artists have the impudence to try and pass off as gems on a discriminating public. Of the value of current coin bearing the impress of her gracious Majesty's head, no Jew, or other money lender is better aware: for all descriptions of precious stones as mounted and displayed in Hancock and Harry Emanuel's windows, I have the keenest appreciation; but still with all due respect to such valuable articles, be it said, there are subjects of conversation more interesting than their origin, age and previous history.

The people who don't understand geology and those other abstruse sciences with unpronounceable names, are mad about music, Florence and Nina West among the number. The other night we had the harp, organ, piano and concertina all going together, and though those instruments are charming in moderation it is quite possible to have too much of a good thing as we found to our cost; another great grievance is our not being allowed to speak during the progress of this combination of sweet sounds: and seeing they commence directly after dinner and continue until one-thirty the next morning, the restriction is severe. In fact where I meant to make new conquests, I find myself under the painful necessity of avowing that our host is the only man worth occupying oneself about; — and he is very difficult to manage, being also affected with the art and music mania. Under pressure of the two, we are made to spend our days in a big tent, where, under the barbarous appellation of an "Eistedfod" [*sic*] a lot of peasants massacre Handel's Messiah, immensely to their own satisfaction; and in a fine art exhibition, entirely got up for the edification of the Welsh nation by the indefatigable Cornwallis: — just as if the poor benighted creatures knew the difference between a Turner and a Claude, without having it pointed out to them. I mildly suggested this, but he wouldn't hear of it at all — it really is very kind of him to take such trouble as he does, to improve these uninteresting savages, who half of them can't even speak English; but such as they are, he is very much attached to them, and in their turn they perfectly idolise him, as indeed they have every reason to. The more I see of them both, the more I am convinced that the best thing the elder brother can do is to die as quickly as maybe; and thus raise this popular regent into the reigning and legal power.

*   *   *   *   *

We left this Sunday, August 9th: Mother goes to Paris to fetch the children back from their school for the summer holidays: Father and I to Leigh where —— is to be invited.

It would be interesting to know which "modern painters" Alice disposes of, here. According to a later description of the house in an auctioneer's catalogue, the family home at Leigh Court, near Bristol, had a collection of "the most eminent Italian, Flemish, Spanish and French masters which would grace the palace of any monarch", and no doubt Alice's education would have included visits to French galleries. As an admirer of Byron she might have accepted Delacroix, but probably would have rejected the earthy Courbet and Millet, and have followed most of the vociferous critics in their ridicule of the early Impressionists. The Pre-Raphaelites she could not have dismissed as "wretched daubs" in view of their meticulous technique, but one wonders how she would have responded to their subject-matter.

Piquant Experiences

FTER her early attempts to interest Cornwallis West, Alice had the good sense to see that she would get nowhere with him, and that even if she had done so, the rarefied atmosphere at Ruthin might not have been to her taste. Never one to waste energy on lost causes, she moved on, anticipating more gratifying experiences at the family's next port of call, Kelham Hall in Nottinghamshire. She had to endure an interim month at Leigh Court, her grandparents' house, during which she contrived with some difficulty, and against opposition from her grandmother, to get Lord Petersham invited to Leigh for September. "The invitation has gone for the 28th, which is all that's most essential," she wrote. "It's a great weight off my mind, for the frights I've had during some of Granny and Mother's stand-up fights, that it would never be sent at all, has rendered my life a perfect burden to me . . . Altogether I shall be more thankful than I can say to get to Kelham and escape for some time from my own thoughts and all these worries. Mother goes with the Baby to Budleigh Salterton to stay with a friend and refresh herself with sea breezes, at least so she says, so the Dear Boy and I will have it all to ourselves."

Alice expected her visit to Kelham to be "very piquant indeed". Clearly, Kelham Hall had a reputation somewhat at odds with the solemn public image generally presented. I trust the present occupiers and loyal local historians will not be too dismayed by Alice's revelations.

Kelham Hall is near Newark in Nottinghamshire, and was acquired by the Newark and Sherwood District Council in 1974. The occupiers at that time were an Anglican missionary order, the Society of the Sacred Mission, who had been in occupation since 1903, after the Manners Sutton family had been forced to sell because of mortgage foreclosure and increased expenses. The District Council takes great pride and pleasure in the house. An admirable booklet, *Kelham Hall: a Family and a House* by Frances Bennett and Gordon Stobbs, has been produced. There are now conference facilities, and rooms can be hired for public or private functions. Grounds and buildings are equally cherished, and the Council generously allows visitors to be shown some of the staggeringly opulent main rooms, by an enthusiastic staff. I was most grateful for the opportunity given to me to do this when I called, quite unexpectedly, rather late on a Friday afternoon.

The present house is probably the third on the site. An earlier house was burnt down in 1857 shortly after it had been expensively refurbished by the rising George Gilbert Scott. Without, it seems, a moment's hesitation, John Henry Manners Sutton, the then owner, set in train the rebuilding of the Hall in the Victorian Gothic style, with a magnificence and opulence rarely equalled. As with many other families, there was strong social pressure on the Manners Suttons to keep up a certain lavish style, which in the end cost them more dearly than they could afford; in fact the money ran out before the building could be completed. In 1862, however, it was ready to accommodate a grand ball, to be held in "the finest ballroom in the kingdom, with ornamental and inlaid floor, groined ceiling and architectural carving". The guests included the Duke of Newcastle, amongst other notables.

An enormous carriage court, which can now accommodate two hundred people, doubled as a conservatory, for the latter never got built. The clock tower never received its clock, and the plans for a proposed grand staircase at the south end were not implemented. Pevsner and Girouard have each commented on this building, which, of a mind-boggling complexity and extravagance, is hard to summarise; but when one recalls that Gilbert Scott was the designer of the Royal Albert Hall and the St Pancras Station Hotel, the flavour of Kelham will be conveyed. Gothic in general inspiration, it is built of red brick, trimmed with other colours, and with patterns in stone and metalwork. Columns, capitals, arches, windows, doorjambs, balustrades, inlaid and tessellated floors — in all of these no opportunity for lavish decoration was lost, and Scott pulled out every stop to achieve richness of effect. Adorned as they would have been with elaborate furniture, carpets, silver plate, porcelain, and paintings, the rooms — including "the mauve bedroom, the pink bedroom, the geranium bedroom, the Catalan bedroom", to name but a few — must have been a vision of luxurious ostentation.

The Cedar Room so much liked by Alice is now a committee room. There is a large stone fireplace with a marble mantelshelf and mirror, and a great three-light mullioned window. The relatively small size of the room and the warm colour and texture of the cedar panelling would have made it a cosy and intimate retreat. It is adorned with fine examples of the Victorian wood-carver's art, the doorways being decorated with carved foliage of many trees — oak, maple, guelder rose, holly and others. The music room, morning room, library and drawing room are all embellished with gilded stonework, transfer patterns of heraldic devices, marble shafts and chimney pieces, inlaid woods and decorative metalwork. The music room balcony or gallery, mentioned by Alice as a vantage point, has ornate carvings and a brass and iron balustrade with leaf and flower forms.

The Manners Sutton family had a long history in the neighbourhood and an Archbishop of Canterbury among their forbears. Their memorials can be seen at Kelham and nearby Averham. When John Henry Manners Sutton attained his majority in 1843 a great feast was prepared for "700 persons . . . who sat down at one o'clock to such a display of good English cheer as has been rarely witnessed". A ball and fireworks followed in the evening. John Henry was elected MP for Newark in 1847 and in 1853 he married Mary (May) Burnaby, sister of Captain Frederick Burnaby. She was Lady Patroness of the Newark Dispensary Ball, and he was Steward of Newark Races. The family presided over the usual feasts, treats and gifts to the children and the poor at Christmas and other ritual occasions. Grand house-parties were given, and inevitably the Prince of Wales was the most notable guest. The Queen's Jubilee in 1887 was celebrated in boats on an ornamental lake; there were also concerts and theatrical performances, for the Manners Suttons had a musical tradition. It is surprising that in the census of 1871 only nine servants were listed as supporting this enormous enterprise, but part-time or temporary help was not included.

In these fantastic "marble halls" Alice, with alert eyes and ears, and impudent tongue, hoped for, and obtained, drama and excitement.

She recommences her diary with renewed inspiration and enthusiasm.

Kelham, Saturday September 5th

Arrived here at about two-thirty, after the most fatiguing journey: and though I have not been in the house twelve hours, have already heaps to write about, whereas a month at Leigh furnished me with no materials.

Edith Wood is installed: quite at home. She goes on the principle of making her friends useful, and has never quitted May since London; and (but this is strictly entre nous) I think May is getting just a little tired of her society. Then there is Mrs Verschoyle; a very pretty brunette of two and thirty, who scarcely looks two and twenty — her husband is a Col. in the Guards; Miss Cator who I met in London, forty and painfully plain, familiarly known as the Camel. Miss Ogle, commonly called "The Ghoul" from a supposed resemblance to that sanguinary creature, who cannot be much more repulsive looking: — she says she's twenty-three: if so, I am very sorry for her, as everyone here puts her on twelve years. Then there's rather a pretty little heiress Miss Harriet Ives Wright, and her mother, who I suspect will put us all in the shade from the mere fact of her possessing £4,000 a year. For the gentlemen there is Mr Creyke or le beau Jésus, so called from his having posed to every modern painter for his heads of Christ; Mr Denison who I met in Paris and took one of those instinctive dislikes to, that so seldom misguide me. I am by no means sorry to meet and study him a little more closely; and last but not least, for he fills a most important role, the individual I alluded to once en passant as destitute of money, appearance, expectations or esprit: Johnny Ogle. This is all at present, but I am happy to say plenty more are coming: Capt. Burnaby is to arrive tomorrow with a brother Blue, and will be warmly welcomed as we are sadly deficient in men.

Now having given the names of the chief actors, let us try to get a little insight into the game they are engaged in, beginning with our fair hostess who plays the first rôle, the others indeed being scarcely more than lookers-on. Now my worthy cousin John Manners Sutton's conjugal principles are, happily for all concerned, constructed of the most elastic and yielding materials and his wife is not slow in turning to the best possible account the liberty she is thus allowed. Indeed, as far as I can make out, the world is quite of the same opinion, May looks upon her lovers as she does upon her dinner: a thing good in itself and indispensable to life; but that to render really palatable, must constantly be varied; since I have known her, and that is barely a twelvemonth, a handsome young Italian, Col. Wynne, Frank Gordon and Baby Stewart whose reign I alluded to in London have all been in turn admitted and dismissed from favour. Yes, dismissed! alas for the poor Baby, his sovereignty has expired and now Johnny Ogle the gambler reigns in his stead. Col. Wynne and au besoin[1] Frank Gordon I can understand; but what May, a woman young, pretty and utterly unscrupulous, can see in her present fancy, everyone is racking their brains to discover. I explain it by the one word "Tricks" [?] and dismiss the subject, just as the gentleman will be himself dismissed, before the rapidly turning autumn leaves have time to fall. I am no particular admirer of les convenances[2], indeed am very much in the habit of putting them quietly aside, when I can do so undetected: but really May's total disregard of them is something alarming.

Tonight for example, when at about one-thirty the ladies had gone to bed, and the gentlemen withdrawn to the enjoyment of cigarettes and tobacco, she begged me to remain up with her a little longer. I complied, and sitting down at the piano, Mr Creyke who I had been studying all night with a view to my own private amusement by my side, ran my hands over the keys and chattered to him; but still keeping a pretty sharp eye on the pair I was supposed to be chaperoning, who whispering on a sofa opposite were up to the

[1]au besoin — at a pinch.
[2]les convenances — the rules of decorum.

present, not quite in each other's arms and that's all I could say. Suddenly May jumped up and said she would sit in the gallery; I followed notwithstanding her remonstrances, not having the slightest idea of being left tête-à-tête with Mr Creyke, at that early hour of the morning: as it was she took care to put the length of the gallery and two folding doors between us. But as they happened to be in glass, and I have an unhappy knack of always turning round at the identical moment my attention ought to be elsewhere, I had ample time and opportunity to take in the tableau they were acting − to keep themselves awake perhaps: certainly it roused me though I was dead asleep. Johnny seated on a low sofa, May on her knees at his feet: both arms round his neck she was slowly drawing down his face on a level with her own. Then their lips met in what seemed to be a prolonged kiss, and I turned away my head, my cheeks the colour of the roses I wore, to meet Mr Creyke's eyes bent inquiringly on mine: he too had taken in the whole scene. "C'est joli!" and he gave his shoulders a little shrug that meant volumes "Dites plutôt que c'est INDIGNE!"[1] and I emphasised the remark, with an indignant rap of my foot on the unoffending carpet. "Que voulez-vous c'est son habitude,"[2] he was going on, when May's voice interrupted us. "Goodnight, Alice, I'm going to bed," and entering her bedroom closely followed by Mr Ogle she precluded any possibility of argument on my part by shutting the door in as matter-of-fact a manner, as if she'd been the most virtuous wife in this virtuous island, accompanied by her legal lord.

This time I was struck perfectly dumb by such audacity − "Goodnight Mr Creyke" was all I said, as I received the candle from his hands "I think it's high time for us to go to bed" and then I went slowly down the gallery towards my room, leaving him to his own reflections on the pretty scene we had just watched enacted; and very flattering conclusions to M—— I should think he must have drawn. Really I cannot wonder at men's disbelieving women's honour, truth and purity, when they come across such examples as these. Pour moi! when I was once in the solitude of my own room, I downright cried with humiliation. It was very stupid on my part, of course, but then I am only seventeen, and not yet accustomed to seeing one of my own sex, and a woman I rather like too, lower herself thus. Then I took off the necklace of pearls I wore and replaced them [deleted] after which [deleted] I went to bed and to sleep [deleted] dreamt [deleted].

[1]Dites plutot . . . Disgraceful's more like it!
[2]Que voulez-vous . . . Oh well, that's how she is.

Kelham Hall: this is the first publication of George Gilbert Scott's drawing of the elevation.

Evening fashions for 1867.
One can see how they allowed
for clever extemporisation
with flowers, leaves and
berries such as Alice enjoyed.

Piquant Experiences

Sunday September 6th

No going to morning church here, as most of us don't summon resolution enough to get up much before ten-thirty, which is rather against attending ten o'clock service. Went however in the afternoon, in the most orthodox manner, and what's more took Mr C—— with me. Of course he was most assiduous in his attentions during our mile walk, but somehow, not withstanding his indisputable good looks, I don't feel myself capable of getting up the smallest interest for him; which is unpleasant in the extreme, seeing there is no one else. However I have great hopes of this Blue who is to arrive tonight. After church May went (doubtless to discuss the sermon) amongst the rector's rose bushes, with J Ogle. Edith Wood and I following heedlessly to ask what was to be done about the carriage found them in a very affectionate attitude indeed: there is nothing like carrying out the very letter of the law, and the excellent discourse we had been listening to, was based on St John's command "Little children love one another". Of course we got rather a sharp dismissal, with a reiteration of the previous order, that we were to take the carriage ourselves and go home. Which we accordingly did: and great was the storm that broke on our devoted heads in consequence; Mrs Verschoyle by this arrangement being left to walk which she resented as a personal insult. Happily for herself, Edith had gone to her room, on coming in, so on me fell the whole weight of her eloquence and really considering the hard and (truth obliges me reluctantly to confess it) unladylike terms used to stigmatise myself and my conduct, I think I stood it very well. Such an exhibition as she made of herself I never saw, stamping her feet, clenching her hands, till she had her audience in fits of laughing: I listening meanwhile in perfect silence, a contemptuous little smile just curling the corners of my mouth, that aggravated her to further abuse and action. The next amusing thing to a scientific flirtation, is to have someone with an ungovernable temper as this little termagant has just showed herself possessed of to rouse and excite at one's own good pleasure. Providence at least up to the present, thought fit to refuse me the one, has granted me the other; and I count on extracting a good deal of quiet innocent enjoyment out of the little lady's tantrums. I began experimenting tonight and found the subject most amenable. Only fancy she gratified me with nearly every adjective in her abusive vocabulary, which is by no means limited, because passing her in the gallery just before dinner, I swept back my skirts disdainfully to avoid her contaminating touch, looking meanwhile with as much sublime unconsciousness over her head, as if totally unaware of the very existence of such an unimportant personage. The rise this little bit of acting got out of her was immense, little Edith[1] came half an hour later in fits of laughter, declaring she never saw anything so well done, and that the fair Clara's remarks were quite as piquant as I intended them to be.

* * * * *

Alas! Alas! such a disappointment; Capt. Burnaby arrived as he said he would, during dinner, but instead of the promised Blue, he brought that little insignificant monkey Tommy Bowles, my last remembrance of whom is the difficulty I had to get rid of him one day in Rotten Row, when I required all my intelligence to be on the qui vive for Lord Lansdowne — And now he turns up here! in the place of that charming young mauvais sujet Lord Carrington. "Blessed are they who expect nothing, for verily I say unto thee they shall in no wise be disappointed." Oh Mahomet! Mahomet! truly those words of yours were dictated by the most profound wisdom and experience of this world and its insidious disappointing ways.

> The "little insignificant monkey" Tommy (properly Thomas Gibson) Bowles was very much underestimated by Alice. He was the founder of *Vanity Fair* and, later, *The Lady*. The centenary number of the latter, in 1985, gave an interesting account of his life and work, and there is a biography of him by Leonard E. Naylor, *The Irrepressible Victorian*, published by Macdonald. Evidently he and Francis Knollys, whom she also dismissed on sight, were short men. Her *beau idéal* was clearly a guards officer of six foot four, and the comparisons she makes between Frenchmen and Englishmen, always in the latter's favour, emphasise the comparative lack of stature of the French. She prided herself on the accuracy of her first impressions, but if such an impression happened to be one of physical "puniness" it was likely to be slapdash rather than accurate.

Monday September 7th

Edith Wood nearly killed me with laughing during the morning, by

---

[1]"Little Edith" is probably the Manners Suttons' thirteen-year-old daughter of that name, not Edith Wood.

dancing the can-can, and telling or inventing more fie-fie stories for my edification. I really don't know in which accomplishment she excels most: no professional danseuse, or scandal-loving old dowager, could beat her at either one or the other. Then Tommy Bowles joined us in the morning room, and read us his latest compositions. He lives by his writing which needless to say is piquant and salé in the extreme: and since he is here, we may as well make up our minds to him, and extract all the amusement we can out of his talents. I am sorry to say that after having given two or three pretty sharp raps to Mrs Verschoyle, of which I watched the effect with great pleasure, I saw myself constrained to make pause, as she apologised for her insolent conduct of yesterday. So there that amusement has deserted me also — Enfin! never despair said the ancients, so I will take courage and trust in what the week may bring forth.

Tuesday September 8th

Before starting for Doncaster races, May called the fairest ones of the ladies together and delivered the following pithy lecture: "My dears, some more men we must have, as we have nothing like enough to look after all these old maids, and Clara and Alice have already taken to fighting in fault of a more profitable occupation. Therefore each of you employ yourselves, in hunting up some one for the good of the community, or yourselves, I'm not particular which, and ask him. Only one condition I make: if it is a married man, he must leave his wife elsewhere, as we have quite enough women. Don't forget and may success attend your efforts. Hush! here come the old maids in question, not a word more," and in very fact the Ghoul and the Camel descended the stairs at the moment, execrably dressed, and by no means fair pictures to look on.

*   *   *   *   *

At his own request Mr Creyke was attached to my especial service that day, which means he was always ready to carry my parasol, run messages, and make himself generally useful. He was with me now, as I turned from the race course to take a critical survey of the company. We had been discussing masculine beauty, and now I singled out a slight handsome man, with a certain look of Cocky, considerably over six foot with large dark eyes, so soft and intensely blue, that they seemed somehow or other as if they ought to belong to a woman.

"There's a face that pleases me," I said, indicating him with a movement of my parasol "He's far and away the best looking man I've seen here today." "Gracious, I know him" was the answer "That's ――; yes, he's very goodlooking, but I won't introduce him to you for he wouldn't amuse you the least: he's a regular man's man – never even looks at a woman – the coldest fellow imaginable." I took no notice of the latter part of Mr Creyke's information, and snubbed him for venturing to suppose that I would allow him to introduce anyone to me, who did not first humbly solicit the favour: – then I left him to go and demolish the wing of a chicken, the luncheon basket being produced, and May raised my spirits by repeating some of the complimentary remarks she, Edith and I were exciting. Mr Creyke came up in the middle of them, and we went back to our former post of observation, then he exclaimed, "By Jove, Miss Miles, you've created an impression on my unimpressionable friend that I never knew any other woman to get. He's trying to be introduced to you." "And who may this friend be?" I asked, knowing perfectly all the time. "Why ―― of course. He came up to me raving about you. 'Creyke my dear fellow, who is that lovely girl you've just been talking to, do introduce me' etc. I never was so surprised in my life. May I fetch him?" I gave the required permission, and five minutes later was chatting merrily with the object of my admiration. He is handsomer than ever when seen at close quarters and very agreeable. Cold? did Mr Creyke say? I'll never believe it with such eyes as those. Of course it occurred to me in course of time that it would be rather pleasant to try the experiment, and have the owner of the eyes still further to enliven lively Kelham: but I thought it too flattering to ask him myself, as May had directed me to; and after due manoeuvering, got Mr Creyke, who is really very convenient, to do it instead. "He won't come though" he assured me. "He doesn't like Mrs M Sutton, and has often refused her invitations. Besides I know he's staying at Lord Halifax." My answer was short, concise and to the point. I had no idea of fatiguing myself refuting all these objections "Do as you're told please, and don't argue the point." So he did as he was told, and Mr ―― said he would be perfectly delighted to come, if only he could manage it with Lord Halifax. "Couldn't you get a telegraph?" I asked demurely, "Of course!" was the answer "That's a most brilliant idea and just what I shall do – so expect me Friday in time for dinner." And so the subject was settled and dismissed, to Mr Creyke's great amazement, and my part in May's directions, fulfilled. Knowing the habits of the house, he told me afterwards, he then went to Mr Denison, and made minute enquiries as to how the party were employed, all leading up to the question "Who is Miss Miles's particular slave?" "Creyke" was the answer. "Does she like him?" "I suppose so." "Then I shan't go," he exclaimed angrily, on which Mr Denison, who, let me give him his due, notwithstanding his bad qualities really behaved very well on that occasion, declared he was only joking, and that so far from liking anyone, I held myself disdainfully apart from all: on hearing which the other was mollified and changed his mind about remaining where he was. Only fancy me coming across Capt. Buckley: he was very uninteresting, not being able to give me any news of his friend.[1] Altogether I spent a very pleasant day, and see my way to spending yet pleasanter ones in the handsome blue-eyed young woman-hater's company. Cold and unimpressionable is he? Why, the being told so I take as a downright defiance, and having at present nothing better to occupy my idle moments, I accept the challenge. Prends garde à toi, mon bel ami! for as surely as you come here Friday night so surely will I try what I can do towards bending to my will, one who has the reputation of never having been spaniel to the fairest woman who ever rendered such captivity captivating.

Thursday 10th September

We went to the races again, the most charming little party, May, Edith and I: with a man apiece, leaving all the proprieties behind, and determined on amusing ourselves lawfully or unlawfully; which we certainly did. To begin with May went off to the grandstand, where we were the only ladies, and surrounded quickly by a crowd of admiring cocottes, who discussed our appearance and dresses in a most audible tone of voice. I insisted on leaving this questionable society, and returning to our own world again, but we were scarcely installed, before Mr Denison arrived with an invitation for us to come and lunch at some dray or other, which we accordingly did, and great fun it was. Again we found ourselves the only ladies in sight and were as such duly appreciated: the master of the dray, an eligible young bachelor whose name I forget, stood bowing and scraping at one window (we had a table laid for us inside, with every delicacy

[1] Lord Petersham presumably, judging from earlier events in London.

available) whilst all his male acquaintances, amused themselves by walking by and staring in at the other. Then he had a celebrated character on whom an admiring public has bestowed the appellation of "Ginger" to sing comic songs for our amusement and finished finally by admiring the races and surrounding country from the top of the dray. Then I saw —— who though I have the misfortune to belong to the weaker sex, didn't at all keep up the reputation he has acquired of avoiding them: quite the contrary. I begin to fear his conquest will not afford half the pleasurable excitement of uncertainty I looked forward to. Didn't reach home till quite late: so Edith and I had our dinner brought into the morning room, feeling too tired and lazy to hurry over an elaborate toilette. A lot of people dined and I should think were rather surprised at seeing us make our appearance, like two good little girls, in the drawing room afterwards.

Friday 11th September

Spent the morning hunting for a trimming for my dress, with Harriet Ives Wright among the rose and ivy bushes, for I am quite resolved to look my very best for Mr ——'s edification and discomfiture: to the furtherance of which I spent the morning gathering materials and Zéphine the afternoon in utilising them. I was amply repaid however for this expenditure of time and trouble, by his start of admiration when I entered the drawing room, purposely late, just before dinner: a cloud of white tarlatane, wings of the same on my shoulders, festooned and trimmed everywhere with trailing ivy sprays, interspersed with clusters of scarlet rose-berries — the same ornaments in my hair. There was a murmur of universal admiration from the women[1] during which I happened to turn to Mr ——: our eyes met: and I being adept at reading their language gave a ~~proudly~~ slightly conscious smile — the projected conquest is certain. The first imperceptible round, thrown from the silken skein, round the strong free hands that later if I so willed it, they could fetter so tightly. But I will take very good care that nothing of the sort shall occur, playing with such sharply pointed instruments as this man's dormant passions, if once fully aroused, would frighten more than amuse me. In cases such as these my just appreciation of physiognomy comes wonderfully to

[1]Was that "murmur" one of unmixed admiration? Or did Alice look like a walking Christmas tree?

my aid, keeping me out of all sorts of mischief, and here it interposes, exclaiming "Thus far shalt thou go and no further" and I shall obey the sage behest, satisfy my vanity by showing this goodlooking untameable young Monster [?] tamed and — no more. All these sage reflections passed through my mind during dinner where I sat by his side — the thing [?] is though to carry them out in practice. We danced as usual during the evening, but somehow or other, I don't know how it was done after the two first valses I found myself seated alone in the cedar room with him where of course we had neither of us the smallest business to be. He didn't say much, compliments not being at all in his line, but looked! — as I should strongly object to anyone looking at my wife if I was a man and had the misfortune to possess such an article, or to anyone looking at me if I was not quite sure of myself, which I am. But even then it gave me a strange sensation not wholly unpleasant and it passed through my head if this is the way people fall in love, I should think the process was a delightful one. Such ideas, though, being strictly unlawful and at utter variance with my principles [deleted] I dismissed them at once and attempted to start some topic of conversation, which righteous effort signally failed on which I folded my hands, put on my most madonna cast of countenance and submitted in silence to be looked at, until my companion could collect his ideas sufficiently to do something else: of which desirable result there did not seem at present to be the most remote probability. His next move was to admire my bracelets, with his eyes still fixed on mine, and his fingers lingering caressingly on my arm. That dodge I am pretty well up to: experience having taught me that men invariably begin making love like that, and really it is not half a bad way of commencing.

*   *   *   *   *

I went to bed very well content with my evening and the progress I had made: Father asking me as we light our candles where I'd been and what I'd been doing all night: I replied innocently "In the cedar room, improving my mind" — a remark that sent both him and Mrs Verschoyle into convulsions of laughter. After all, what was I doing but taking a lesson in the stability of the strongest of human resolutions, when exposed to fire.

Every Girl's Duty

Saturday 12th September

Coming down to breakfast this morning at my usually late hour, I found Mr —— waiting for me at the foot of the stairs, an attention he repeated every other morning. That I call pretty well, from a man utterly unaccustomed to offer the least petit soins. I had a fine fire made in the cedar room and sat over it all the morning with him as my companion: the other gentlemen were out shooting but for the first time in his life this enthusiastic young sportsman discovered there might be game more worth pursuing than partridges and gave up the one the better to study the other: so as I did not happen to be in the mood for going out we remained most domestically au coin du feu, I leaning back in the most luxurious of easy chairs, warming the tips of my coquettish black satin shoes, talking on every subject imaginable: his own affairs among the number. It appears he has the dearest old father he is perfectly devoted to, and who is constantly making the following admirable remark — "When you want to marry, —— my dear boy, you have only to tell me so, and I will turn out at once for you and your wife." A most charming idea and I only wished all elderly gentlemen professed it. The question is, would he ever have the strength of mind to put it into execution?

I began a letter to Minnie just before luncheon, and looking over my shoulder Clara Verschoyle read aloud the definition I was giving of the company. " 'We have four beauties, one heiress, the usual sprinkling of London men, and an inordinate amount of detrimentals' — Under which latter clause I suppose you are included, Mr ——" she added maliciously and as I did not occupy myself contradicting her, he concluded I believed it, and took great trouble to prove the contrary that afternoon, as in a deliciously idle mood we were loitering about the garden, nominally to make the gentlemen bouquets. "I began life as a detrimental," he said, twisting some geraniums about and giving me a side-long glance to see if his words took due effect. "But thank Heaven that's over, and I can assure you I find life much pleasanter as an eligible." "Isn't that pretty?" and I held up a completed bouquet: then when he had expressed his admiration — "I can quite believe the world is a pleasant place if you have plenty of money" I said carelessly "it making the man, in so many people's idea, though myself I never could see it made the smallest possible difference." And having delivered myself of this fine sentiment, so utterly at variance with my whole code of morals, I bent my face over the flowers in my lap and became straightway absorbed in the manufacturing of another bou-

62

quet, leaving only the back of my head for his contemplation. "I never saw such glorious hair if it is all real" a little doubtfully. "That is about the third time you have expressed yourself uncertain about it" I said indignantly, "you most irreclaimable of unbelievers. Why, Judas Iscariot was nothing to you." "There is a very easy manner of convincing me: do let me see it down some night" he pleaded "as even the Holy Scriptures condemn those who hide their light under a bushel, and bury their talent in the earth." After a due expenditure of insinuating speeches I allowed myself to be persuaded into giving a half promise, that in the next favourable opportunity, his wish should be gratified. "I'm most dreadfully matter of fact" he declared "and like irrefutable evidence. I had another doubt about you at the races; but that is entirely gone." "Voyons! what other enormity did you imagine I practised?" "One of the most unpardonable of all, that of painting your eyes" then as I threw up those calumniated orbs in horror "You needn't be angry, for I assure you, they look exactly like it, as you have naturally that dark look about them women paint to obtain; and contrasting with your golden hair and fair white skin, it is still more remarkable." I laughed at this candid remark: really for such a very innocent young man he seems to me to be singularly clear-sighted concerning these little roueries[1] of women. I told him so, winding up by remarking "you were represented to me as a species of civilised savage shunning above all things women, however fascinating, and their society" then with a coquettish lowering of my eyes and voice "I don't find you so at all." "You are the first person who has ever found me otherwise," he remarked, taking possession of the hand nearest him (a most unnecessary movement) and stroking it caressingly "And most probably the other ladies here would say the same; why, not only have I not spoken to them, but I don't even know all their names." "And what makes you so disagreeable generally?" I asked looking innocently up into the eyes turned so appropriatively on mine. "Because I think a man ought to be a man, and not the slave of the caprices of any pretty woman who, to occupy some idle moments the world or her dressmaker have not engrossed, will try and turn him into a spaniel, with the sole object of passing her time. Notwithstanding which fine sentiments I am ready to be your spaniel or retriever or whatever other thing you like, for as long as you will consent to keep me." "Retriever then it shall be!" I said gaily "Consider yourself rechristened." "Only try me!" he said smiling "I shall always answer to

[1]Roueries — stratagems or wiles.

the name. Whistle even if you want me." "But I don't know how!" I said, making a faint trial which signally failed; then he tried to teach me, and we laughed a good deal over the lesson.

* * * * *

I never knew anything so presumptuous as little Tommy Bowles has grown. He has taken it into his head to be personally aggrieved at ——'s pretty attentions and my gracious manner of accepting. Just as if anything I elect to do can by any possibility be any concern of his. However he is of a different opinion and has said two or three things of the most jealous impudent description imaginable, to me, not being the least subdued by the snubbing he received. Tonight he thought fit to bear down on the half of the sofa I was reserving for my favourite, but I saw through his intentions, and before he had time to carry them into execution, by one of those dexterous twitches of the hand I have lived too long in Paris not to be perfect mistress of, my dress that had been reposing quietly on the floor, now covered the vacant seat with clouds of mist-coloured tulle and violet and white chrysanthemums. Mr ——'s face of amusement and Tommy's expression of discomfiture as I deftly executed that movement, were a perfect caution. "I quite understand your manoeuvre!" the latter remarked in a tone he meant to be bitterly sarcastic, "but it shall profit you nothing. Will you be kind enough to dispose of all that drapery elsewhere and make room for me to sit down." I looked at him perfectly amazed, as well I might be, at such audacity. "Most unquestionably no, I shall do nothing of the kind. My dress looks infinitely better there than ever you would, and there it shall remain." But he was not to be done so easily: pulling up a chair as near as he could, he installed himself at my side; and the difficulty I had in getting rid of him, no one would believe. At last I had the brilliant idea of despatching him up to his room, in search of a book he inadvertently admitted to having left there. Of course long before he came down again, my retriever sauntered up, and the petticoats that so suddenly expanded, as magically diminished, and he sunk down into the coveted place, languidly remarking, "I don't move that little beggar's chair because I want to see if he'll have the audacity to take possession of it again now I'm here." Which audacity I'm happy to say the little beggar had not, a diabolical scowl being the only notice he vouchsafed me as he presented me with the book, which I received most graciously, acting on the truly Christian principle of turning away evil by good.

Sunday 13th September

Ate my breakfast with my retriever installed as head waiter, to take care I had everything that was good, and having at length dawdled away an incredibly long space of time over the wing of a partridge, set off with him, half an hour late. As the service was at Aram,[1] needless to say we never arrived. Kelham churchyard we found quite sufficient for our religious feelings and there we loitered away half the morning, reading the inscriptions on the tombs, searching among the long grass for some finer sorts useful to me in making up the gentlemen's bouquets; and talking sentiment, much as the poor dead people laying [*sic*] there had done too in their day. We buried a swallow in this consecrated ground pronouncing a very pretty little funeral oration over him, and then Mr —— returned to the gardens, got some flowers and grapes and selecting a nice sunny spot sat down to enjoy ourselves therewith. To say nothing of it being a very pretty employment, as a pretext, this making bouquets for the gentlemen is quite invaluable to me. Now, they gave me full occupation till lunch time; while my retriever lay stretched his lazy length on the grass besides me, watching me in a manner that made a picture I saw of Samson and Delilah recur forcibly to my memory. I went to afternoon church, as Mr —— had business in Newark, and then on his return we sat with a game of solitaire between us, till six-thirty when I always go to my room as I hate having to hurry myself over dressing.

*   *   *   *   *

I will say May is very good in this: every night he takes me into dinner and under his care it is far from being the least pleasant part of the day. "You are just like one of those pretty tropical birds pecking at their food!" he informed me tonight. "The daintiest little lady my experience has ever brought me into contact with." "Oh, your experience" and I paused with a walnut glacé in tempting proximity to my mouth "your experience and of women too, 'M. le sauvage'." But my saucy speech in no wise disconcerted him. "Yes, my experience. You may laugh if you please, and as you doubtless know, laughing is very becoming to you; but because I don't choose, after the example of

---

[1]Alice's spelling of Averham, perhaps based on local pronunciation. Averham is two or three miles from Kelham Hall. Kelham Church is in the Hall's grounds.

the rest of my sex, to be made a fool of by every pretty woman who takes it into her head to try the experiment, is no reason that I shouldn't observe, and I'm a great observer!" "And might I be so bold as to enquire the result of the profound cogitations concerning myself?" I asked, having disposed of the walnut, and raising two mocking eyes to him. "I have told you: you are the daintiest little lady possible to meet, I delight in watching the disdainful manner in which you nibble the most recherché dishes, du bout des dents[1], and a physiognomist would read your whole character in the way you eat a grape." "How?" I enquired laughing "I don't promise to correct myself, but still I like to know my failings." "To me it's no failing," was the answer "I delight in watching you make two or three deliberate mouthfuls of the tiny fruit instead of swallowing it at once as anyone else would. You throw a peculiar refinement of your own into this most ordinary process that always irresistibly reminds me of the old Bible story and our mother Eve, I am sure just as now you eat the grape, with the same dainty precautions and lazy enjoyment, she centuries ago ate the apple." I laughed at this original comparison. "I really shall have to guard my conduct, under the eyes of such an observer"; and then May gave the signal for the ladies retiring, and after the slight confusion consequent on moving, and the general rush of devoted slaves under the table for their respective sovereigns' gloves and handkerchiefs, we found ourselves in the cedar room, and after having taken every disposition for comfort, some grouped round the fire, the rest on sofas or chaises longues, the usual badinage on each others' affairs and choice bits of scandal began, that, at houses like Kelham, supersede the usual after-dinner conversations on fine little boys and girls and surmises as to who will or won't next. "It appears Lady Holmesdale is still toqué[2] about her little officer!" May announces languidly from the sofa, "and Lord Holmesdale has telegraphed for three detectives." There is a general cry of "Shame, shame," and then it occurs to someone to ask "what for?" "To look after her Ladyship's morals I suppose," Clara suggested. "Say her £30,000 a year," I corrected. "Thanks, Doughty, no coffee, only some sugar and cream."

[1]du bout des dents − literally "with the tip of the teeth", meaning toying with food.
[2]Toqué − crazy.

Alice goes on to report a couple of pages of this gossip, taking care to include a spiteful jibe of Clara Verschoyle's which she herself promptly outdoes, and an admiring remark of May's on the subjugation of the "Retriever". Then someone comes quietly into the cedar room.

Harriet exclaimed "Goodness me! What's that!" and all the ladies started into strict propriety, from the graceful abandon of their attitudes — all but May, who never yet disturbed herself for mortal man, and myself, who, conscious that the tip of my pink satin shoes visible were coquetry personified, also that buried in the cushions of that deep arm chair, my feet up on another, made a much prettier picture, than sitting bolt upright as if under arms in a brilliantly lighted drawing room, instead of the delicious demi-lumière of this sleepy little boudoir, where a certain licence is not only permitted, but almost required; third and the strongest reason of all, I had recognised the intruder, before the others even perceived him, and was inclined to give him the full benefit of the tableau. Need I say it was my retriever? A chorus greeted him "Mr ——!" in every tone of amazement. "Yes, it's me[1] it is I" he answered quite coolly drawing a chair up as close to mine, as it could be persuaded to go — "They've begun to talk politics in there" pointing to the dining room — "and that I know is interminable; so I just took my audacity in both hands, and joined the ladies. Do you think I shall be forgiven?" he asked, his voice softening as he turned to me, and I would have found it in my heart to give him a kiss on the spot, in gratitude for the attention and signal victory I thus carried off, before so many witnesses. Later when he began to worry about my hair again, I really thought he deserved a reward for his bit of gallantry, and after a great expenditure of words and entreaties, allowed an unwilling permission to be coaxed out of me, to his waiting, in the Galerie des Dames, half an hour after the ladies had retired.

* * * * *

The clock struck one as we went upstairs to bed; — unusually early. "Come into my room for a little with me, Alice dear," Edith said passing her arm caressingly through mine "I want to ask your advice

---

[1] Alice's grammar sometimes falters, but her admirer's is not allowed to. The correction is hers.

about something, and read you the letter I've been composing to Francis Knolls" but excusing myself on the grounds of a headache, I went out to my own room, and letting down my hair I gave it as slow and deliberate a brushing as if I had no other occupation in view. Having wasted sufficient time over this pastime, to let the house get quiet, and inspire —— with serious doubts as to my coming at all, I made up my mind to relieve his suspense, and candle in hand, advanced bravely enough to the Gallery, though feeling shyer than I should have thought myself capable of doing under any possible circumstances; but in this charming house there are looking-glasses everywhere and the glimpse I caught of myself in passing one; — clouds of mist-coloured drapery and pretty face faintly flushed with excitement, looking prettier than ever, framed in the masses of tawny golden hair (that begins in Belgravia and ends in Tyburnia, as Augustus used to say during our séances) the bright candlelight held in dangerous proximity throwing a glow over all; — went far to reassure me: and ——'s advance from the other end of the Gallery as handsome as a picture in his picturesque smoking costume[1] of some dark coloured velvet; — put retreat entirely out of the question. "Thanks so much for coming": — a dead pause, and then with a sigh of admiration "I never saw anything so glorious!" that was all he said, this undemonstrative young man, where others would have seized the opportunity to pay 1,000 compliments: but he looked: I can only compare the glances I was favoured with, to the expression I should invest [?] a Royal Bengal Tiger with, waiting for the moment to dart on his prey. I won't say I was alarmed, having too much confidence in myself for the indulgence of any such puerile emotion, but still I began to think seriously of beating a retreat, and was quite thankful, upon my approaching incautiously too near the balustrade, that provoking Denison, who seems to have my singular facility of being in the wrong place at the wrong moment, catching sight of my unbound hair from below, called to me to come down and rehearse Desdemona en costume for the tableau we are to act, I left —— and went. As I wished him goodnight, he tried very hard to put his arm round my waist, when I think, notwithstanding his virtue and my good Resolutions, it would have been wished in quite a different manner; but though not perhaps violently averse in my heart, I was much too

---

[1]The smell of tobacco was offensive to ladies, so after-dinner smoking was done in smoking rooms, wearing special jackets, usually of velvet, and caps.

politic to allow of any such demonstration: men are such brutes, you never can allow them the tiniest little favour without losing somewhat in their esteem; − and when Mr —— looks back on my memory, if he looks back at all, I intend him to be able to elevate it on a pedestal, and invest it with all the halo of the unattainable and unknown; for alas, for weak human nature, it would be only waste of time and breath to try and convince even the most intelligent among the sons of men, that the humble daisy peeping from the grass at their feet, is in anywise equal to the beautiful golden apple swinging so temptingly above their head, just out of reach of their uplifted hand. The moral of all this is, that our goodnight might have been witnessed by the whole house, and I went down to take my place in the tableau in question, with a quiet conscience, though perhaps with just a shade brighter colour in my cheeks, than the pace at which I descended the stairs, strictly warranted.

Notwithstanding his fancied grievances Tommy Bowles couldn't help regarding me with a certain reluctant approval, ludicrous in the extreme. Then coming up to me he launched the following, in the most sarcastic tone he could command − "Allow me to offer you my respectful sympathy, Miss Miles, on the absence of the only person for whom these beautiful locks are given their liberty!" and he lifted up a long tress of hair, "I cannot but pity him, though his loss is our gain." Which remark, coupled with my lively recollection of the foregoing scenes, sent me into such a fit of laughter, as greatly to discompose my impudent little adversary, who concluded such merriment was not without cause, and vaguely perceived he'd been ridiculous, which was the more aggravating, as he couldn't quite tell how!

Altogether I think I may mark this as a most amusing and eventful evening.

Monday September 14th

The whole party went off on an expedition to some forest[1] or other, with a view, I believe, to improving their minds, by the contemplation of Lord Manners' new house: all but Clara Verschoyle who had a headache, May, Johnny Ogle, my retriever and I, [who] stayed at home, with the intention of occupying ourselves in an entirely

---

[1]Presumably Sherwood Forest.

different manner. I can't pretend to say what May did: seeing she disappeared directly after breakfast and was no more seen till luncheon, repeating the performance as soon as that meal was concluded. I sat over the cedar room fire, lazily discussing matrimony with Mr —— and making him tell me of the very few flirtations he ever indulged in, and which being more the work of circumstance than will, and from the height of the science to which I have attained I look disdainfully on, and don't call flirting at all. I put on an alpine,[1] the weather having turned out quite cold, and we walked to Aram during the afternoon. Our last walk! how well I remember it! We sat down under such shelter as a bank and an old hollow tree afforded, he holding my hand that he had taken nominally to warm, and didn't relinquish, looking at me with that appropriative glance I have no sort of objection to when coming from such fine eyes, assuming my most madonna cast of countenance and my eyes bent on the ground and said nothing at all: silence often being more expressive than the wittiest conversation. "It is very wearisome to have to go back to real life and work tomorrow!" he said at last with a sigh. "No words can say how much I have enjoyed this holiday – thanks to you," to which I responded softly that I was delighted he found such pleasure in my society, and that I hoped we might meet each other again later: which of course we shan't. People utterly and entirely indifferent to you, I remark, are forever turning up when they are least expected, whereas there always seems to be a sort of fate preventing you seeing those you really took a fancy to: and a great fancy I have taken to Mr —— , everything in him pleases me, even down to his incredibly candid remarks. "I wish you wouldn't let that child go on kissing you so much," he said abruptly this morning, after Edith[2] had been coaxing me even more than usual. "Why not?" I asked innocently. "Because it's absurd, doesn't afford you the slightest satisfaction, and provokes me!" "How?" "By exciting ideas you could not understand, and I need not enter into." "No, indeed, you are right," I said laughing "such ideas are quite beyond my limited comprehension" and we let the subject drop, passing on to another, that of my hair. "From the hesitation and timidity you evinced, in letting me only see it," he said, "I should have imagined you thought you were committing some great enormity; whilst when that bothering Denison called you, you went

[1] A warm cloak.
[2] Edith: this is certainly Edith Manners Sutton.

"Psyche", by Greuze, had been in Lord Hertford's collection for some time when Alice was in London, and was probably among the paintings Augustus Lumley had seen. The pose he chose for Alice sounds like Psyche's — with modifications in the interests of modesty.

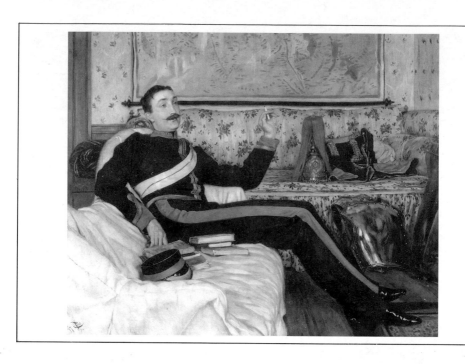

Above: Frederick Gustavus Burnaby in 1870, by J.G. Tissot.
Below left: "Cocky" – Henry Charles Keith Petty Fitzmaurice,
5th Marquess of Lansdowne. Right: The Earl of Harrington –
Viscount Petersham when Alice knew him.

Caricatures by "Spy" of Tommy Bowles and Sir Francis Knollys; and Giovanni Boldini's portrait of Lady Colin Campbell, cousin of Alice's mother who was a key witness in her defence in the divorce court.

Hollingbourne House: the east front and the drawing room in Alice's time.

down into the midst of all those people in the cedar room, with as much sublime indifference, as if they never existed!" "Yes, but that was quite another thing!" and left him to digest this bit of feminine logic, as best he might. "It's not seven," he called after me reproachfully, "and the bell won't ring for another hour. If you go and dress now, you will be ready ever so long before dinner. In that case, come down will you, instead of sitting over that french novel upstairs?" "I'll see about it!" I answered laughing, and went to my room determined to hasten Zéphine's nimble fingers: — she met me with the pleasant comment "Mlle has no flowers." "And the ones I saw here this morning?" I enquired. "All dead except these" and she held up some geraniums of a delicate shade of pink "they would look lovely in Mlle's hair, if Mlle would send out for some." "Mr —— can go I suppose," I said more to myself than to her, "I certainly can't in my dressing gown and with all my hair down. Besides what on earth is the good of having a retriever, if you wait upon yourself." — with which reflection I took the flowers and went into the gallery. On looking down into the music hall, I was not best pleased at seeing him engaged in earnest conversation with Clara, who, although we are very good friends now, I still think a mischievous little thing enough, quite ready to give me the length and breadth of her tongue, whenever a fitting opportunity presents itself. She had one now, and I more than suspect, was working out her ideas respecting me, for Mr —— 's benefit, entirely to her own satisfaction, when I cut short her innocent little diversion by throwing down the flowers to be matched, and he departed with what must have seemed to her the most unnecessary promptitude to do my bidding. "I really wish, Alice, you wouldn't send Mr —— on errands when he is talking to me" she exclaimed in an annoyed tone of voice, on which I retaliated "Really, Clara, if you want someone all to yourself make the conquest by your own unaided powers, and I will respect it; but I've not the smallest idea of putting myself to any inconvenience, because it amuses you, tampering with my goods!"

Really this is the most extraordinary house, and its mistress's conduct the queerest part about it. When Mr —— returned with my flowers, he met May at the bottom of the stairs, and enquired of her very naturally, how he was to get them delivered to me, on which she said with the greatest nonchalance "I suppose you are capable of taking them to her yourself: go straight upstairs along the gallery and the first room on the first turning to the right is Alice's. What are you standing staring at me like that for, I can't be more explicit in my directions." "But Mrs Sutton" the poor young man began, quite confused, "I couldn't really think of doing such a thing: —" when little Edie appeared and came to the rescue by exclaiming "Give the flowers to me, Alice said I was to wait for them." She brought them up and recounted the foregoing conversation for my benefit, winding up with "Isn't it extraordinary how Mother can take pleasure in making such a fool of herself."

> We now approach the moment when Alice will forget discretion and betray her Retriever's name. She will sometimes revert to using a dash, but I shall continue to use his name, which was George Morland Hutton. Later in the diary Alice provides further clues, enabling me to run him to earth. He was born on December 3rd 1834, and became Lord of the Manor of Gate Burton, Knaith and Wallingham in Lincolnshire. Alice notes that his conduct during the Crimean War (he served in the 46th Foot) was "gallant" and that he was present at the taking of Sebastopol in 1855. He became a JP, and a Captain of the Royal North Lincolnshire Militia. When Alice uses his name she spells it Moreland.

Going downstairs as I said I would, a little after the dressing bell rung, for Zéphine's fingers had been most expeditious and Edie's chatter had not made me late, I found Mr —— waiting for me by the cedar room fire. I sat down on a stool to warm myself before it, and by this delicious flirting [?] light (I am happy to say no one offered to bring candles) we remained chatting till the others began to make their appearance. Moreland's greatest friend Tommy Eyre as he calls him, who only arrived this afternoon was one of the first to come down, and he straightway began reproaching my retriever for not having gone to his room as he had promised to do when dressed. Mr Hutton began some lame excuse about having completely forgotten it during which the other looked at me and coupling my slightly sceptical smile with the little tableau he had disturbed by his abrupt entrance, a very simple one too, for it was only Moreland clasping my bracelet, out of which little act of politeness, my relations themselves could scarcely have tortured materials for a moral lecture: smiled in his turn and drew his own conclusions.

The band came over from Newark and we danced until three o'clock in the morning. I am happy to state that my retriever valses as well as — as — well as he stares. May was more insupportable than I have ever known her, which is saying a good deal. The way she ran after us, and chased us about the whole evening, showed an infinite want of tact, almost of good breeding. I got downright angry at last, and rated her soundly, to Moreland's great amusement, suggesting that if she minded her own manners and her own business, it would be a great deal better for all parties, which excellent advice I am sorry to say she did not take. Quarrelled just a little with my retriever too, and went to bed before the ball was over, nervous and hysterical without the least knowing why, leaving him in despair, fearing he had overwalked me today.

Tuesday September 15th

I spent the morning roaming round the garden and the conservatory, when notwithstanding his contempt for all such practices, Moreland actually forgot his ideas sufficiently to kiss my hand, after buttoning my glove for me. I flatter myself that by this time I am pretty well accustomed to receiving with the most superb indifference all such salutes yet even I, found his manner of doing it, and solemn earnest eyes, rather embarrassing. My dear good faithful retriever! He left at two-thirty, and I declare I was almost as sorry as I should be if some shower of rain came and spoilt my tiniest most becoming bonnet. He couldn't help going, however, as some friends came to his house today, that he specially invited, and having gone I put his image carefully away into a corner of my memory to be reproduced over at Leigh, as here my time is too short and consequently precious to be wasted in the indulgence of any such weakness. First, and by way of doing a little stroke of business I devoted myself to his friend,[1] who I told May to give me as a cavalier at dinner, and won over at once. There is nothing like having a man's greatest friend devoted to your interest. You may never require his services, it is true, but again it is possible a case might occur where he would be very useful, and where even securing his neutrality would be most important to your success. Anyhow don't neglect the opportunity of making his conquest, and I really found Col. Eyre very amusing. His astonishment at what he is pleased to term "Moreland's bewitcher" is something comic. "You can't appreciate it," he informed me, "for you don't know him. Now notwithstanding my affection for him I must own he is a regular savage with regard to the ladies, never can be brought to appreciate

[1]Colonel Eyre — Tommy Eyre, as Morland Hutton calls him.

their charms, than if they were totally devoid of them, so imagine my surprise on arriving here, ready as much to remonstrate with him, rather finding him as he himself informed me, duly installed as your pet retriever and most devoted slave. What his mother will say when she hears of it, as she certainly will, I don't know!" "Why? What harm was he doing?" "None, but she, with all due respect be it said, is the most insupportable woman I ever met during the thirty-three years I have been knocking about the world. She has a mortal fear of his marrying that leads her to encourage him in his avoidance of the fair sex, and if she hears of him speaking to any girl it disturbs her innocent slumbers for a week. A pleasant life anyone would have with her, beautiful capricious exacting termagant!" That would be a pleasant sort of woman to have for a mother-in-law I thought, but did not say; and Col. Eyre went on lauding up his friend, his honourable chivalrous nature, gallant conduct in the Crimea, with many other details, until I declare I was quite impressed. During this conversation we were sitting in the cedar room, doing chaperone to May and Johnny Ogle, lolling on a sofa opposite. At the end of about twenty minutes spent without any unusual infringement of decorum, May jumped up, and declaring it would be much [more] pleasant with only the firelight, turned down the lamp as low as she possibly could without actually putting it out. "Is that quite prudent, my dear?" I asked. "What on earth would Manners say if he came in?" But "Bother Manners" was the only reply my caution elicited, so I moved back my chair a little from Col. Eyre's which I thought unnecessarily close, and returned to the theme of my retriever's merits without taking any further notice of the delinquents opposite. My companion however, not being equally used to their peculiar proceedings, did keep his eyes occasionally on them, and nearly died of laughing, when Johnny, saying something about the fire being in May's eyes, dexterously introduced a screen between us, which manoeuvre had scarcely been executed, when in walked the injured husband. Now John Manners Sutton professes with far too much orthodoxy the morals of the high society in which he moves, not to be completely above manifesting that passion so prevalent among the lower orders, viz; jealousy. Wherefore, though he took in the state of affairs at one glance, it was with the most perfectly gentlemanlike and aristocratic indifference that he moved towards the lamp with the evident intention of turning it up. But alas! for human intentions! Si l'homme propose, femme dispose — and May had lowered the wick with such methodical nicety, also the peculiar genius that always does seem to protect all ladies under these sort of emergencies, now influenced her husband's hand, he gave it the tiniest switch the wrong way, but it was sufficient. The flickering flame went out, and we were left in total darkness save for the uncertain firelight, which Manners went and poked rather viciously till he succeeded in producing the tiniest flame. As for Col. Eyre, this time he could stand it no longer, and his laughter was perfectly audible, notwithstanding the pillow in which he had buried his face. Nothing is so infectious as mirth, so I take great credit to myself for keeping my countenance under all these difficult circumstances. Col. Eyre goes tomorrow morning long before I shall have opened my eyes to the day and the business awaiting me. I am really very sorry, for he is most amusing, though perhaps a little audacious. I looked over his shoulder today and saw the most absurd sketch of my retriever kneeling at my feet, done in the style of Lear's book of Nonsense,[1] and written under it:

> I have a friend called Moreland Hutton
> Who swore that he cared not a button
> For women fair and their wiles
> Till lovely Miss Miles
> Taught him better at John Manners Sutton.

He then threw it into the fire when he saw me looking over his shoulder but not before I had had time to read it.

Owing to my own affairs I have been greatly neglecting the general public lately, so now I suppose I had better touch on them en passant.

Lots of men have come and gone, making place to others, the number of ladies has been only augmented by a Miss Shiel who I think very young and pretty to be allowed the unlimited liberty she seems to enjoy. Harriet Ives Wright and I are the greatest friends and her mother charming: her ideas of propriety just a little too stiff, perhaps, but after all what can you expect from a person passing half their life up in the Scotch wilds with its primitif morals. Besides it's a very fine thing to err on the right side and I sincerely wish I could do it myself, which I can't — However hard I try I never can manage to be shocked at my neighbours' misdemeanours, or look on them at all as my affairs, which of course is very wrong indeed and proving a want of principles dreadful to have to state; what it proceeds from I can't

[1]Edward Lear's *Book of Nonsense* was published in 1846.

imagine! Unless perhaps from my peculiar bringing up; mais enfin, c'est comme cela, and all indulgent and naughty as I am, dear good Mrs Ives Wright is kind enough to be very fond of me.

Alice, having succeeded in attracting Morland Hutton, became "the biter bit" and found herself genuinely attracted by him — though she tried to persuade herself that he ought to be richer. She also learned that he had a formidable mother, who did *not* plan for him to marry. He departed, nothing was resolved, and Alice looked elsewhere for diversion and a new slave to pander to her wishes. Fate handed her Sir John Metcalfe (1828–1883). He was in the Indian Civil Service, but at the time of the Indian Mutiny (1857) his knowledge of the country was of great service to the army. The *Dictionary of National Biography* calls him a "brave and resolute man". He was hated and feared by the natives and had a price on his head. Made a CB in 1864, he retired on an invalid pension in 1866. His first wife Charlotte died in 1851. He married again in 1876.

[no date]

Sir John Metcalfe, the great Indian hero, has just arrived à point to divert my thoughts from my retriever's merits, about which, being past, I need no longer occupy myself. We have all had our curiosity sufficiently excited about the baronet by the stories which preceded him: as far as I can make out at present he has the good taste to be, or feign to be, immensely smitten by my beaux yeux, against which indeed, as far as he's concerned, not the shadow of an accusation can be lodged, as they were entirely differently occupied. That occupation however having taken its departure simultaneously with my handsome friend, I don't see the smallest inconvenience in promoting to his place this by no means unwilling Indian hero. It will be a contrast to Moreland certainly, as he looks about forty-six, and has only one eye, otherwise il n'est pas mal and then contrast is so piquant! Besides it's morally impossible that I can do without someone to run messages, carry my flowers, and otherwise be at my entire disposal. Since pages went out, retrievers as a natural result came in, but though he shall fill the capacity I won't call him by that name, which for the future is sacred to Moreland. Tonight — and how I have been wandering from tonight to be sure, was Mr Creyke's play "All is fair in Love or War" a motto soit dit en passant, that has my entire approval. Afterwards my tableau[1] of Desdemona in which with my eyes closed, dishevelled hair, and a becoming white peignoir, I looked infinitely better than ever did the Moor's virtuous little wife — at least so the discriminating public was kind enough to inform me: Sir John being speaker and admirer in chief. When I came back in my ball dress, my hair still à la Madeleine, and vouchsafed him a valse the conquest was quite completed. Oh dear! oh dear! what idiots men are to be sure. A bit of flesh and blood rather more prettily painted than her sisters is quite sufficient to turn their heads! and if peradventure they see a girl with soft eyes, glossy hair, and a skin like milk and roses, they at once jump to the conclusion she's an angel — instead of reflecting that probably her mother sees to her being in bed every night at ten-thirty, and she has a decided taste for good healthy mutton chops, which two prosaic things have a great deal more influence on the appearance than any angelic quality of mind. Besides I remark that those women who could properly be styled angels, are invariably plain. Tout se compense.

Saturday September 19th

My pleasant visit is drawing very near its termination; but I still have any amount to write. To begin with my own affairs. Sir John the redoubted Indian hero, before whose relentless sword and iron will 700 sepoys went down, and who only regrets not having slain instead a 1,000, Sir John, whose name is cited as a miracle of courage, skill, successful daring, Sir John has succumbed, yielded up his colours and himself, rescue or no rescue, tied bound prisoner at the feet of "Sweet seventeen" who to tell the truth is somewhat perplexed about what to do with her conquest. Whatever can have possessed him to take my pretty smiles and words given as freely to the lowest peasant, so much au sérieux, I can't conceive, for to treat him as I did Moreland never even entered my mind, and I was only a shade more gracious than to the general public; which share, falling on his masculine vanity, was quite sufficient to turn his head, for turned it must have been to allow of his for one moment entertaining the preposterous idea, that I was ready to sacrifice my whole life and youth and beauty to him: and all

[1]The silent and static *tableau* was a form of amateur theatricals favoured by pretty young women who could not be expected to memorise dialogue. They simply posed in representations of historical or allegorical subjects.

on the strength of my having accepted his attentions — faute de mieux — for a few days during which time I must own I hadn't much fault to find with him. He's a confirmed atheist, but concealed his opinions very carefully for fear of shocking my high moral feeling (s'il savait seulement comme cela m'est égal!)[1] accompanying me to church on Sunday and repeating all the responses in the most orthodox manner: then he carried my flowers as carefully as Moreland himself, and told me far more amusing stories than ever my retriever indulged in: but — somehow or other, it was not the same thing: and at the end of one or two trials I became so thoroughly convinced of it, that I gave up my favourite occupation, and the gentlemen had to do without their favourite bouquets. Zephyr having departed, Flora (as he used to call me) forsook for the nonce her flowers. One day I was inveigled into going out with Sir John and Edith [Wood] in the boat: but that capricious young damsel, catching sight of Manners, a particular admirer of hers, taking a solitary walk, was seized with a sudden fit of compassion and insisted on being put ashore to join him, therefore we had the felicity of a tête-à-tête row home. Needlessly to say Sir John went as slowly as possible, and thinking of the cheerful fire and amusing book awaiting me chez nous, I could have cried with cold, disgust and vexation. However all ordeals come to an end in this world, and so did this aquatic excursion of ours: needless to say I registered a mental vow, never under similar circumstances to undertake another. Sir John can scarcely be aware of my charitable resolution to judge from his conduct tonight: I never saw a man make a much greater fool of himself: and I have seen plenty of them behave in a most ridiculous manner too. I have no sort of objection to his staring: and even kissing my hand, respectfully and in moderation: — but I really think the way in which he did it tonight was most unnecessary: he almost hurt me in the tumult of his feelings.

One amusement I do get out of him and his proceedings; a very harmless one, and yet — such is the rebellious and froward disposition of mankind — an amusement he would probably greatly object to: that of my talking him over with Clara every night. As I was going to her room as usual at about twelve-thirty I caught a glimpse of our fair hostess on her way upstairs to pay Johnny Ogle the usual nocturnal visit: there was nothing uncommon in this proceeding, and yet when remarking on it to Clara, I couldn't repress some words of alarm.

[1] s'il savait seulement . . . If he only knew how little I cared!

"Why, what on earth is the matter, Alice?" she asked, putting back the thick tresses of brown hair off her pretty face to look at me. "You ought to be pretty well accustomed to May's eccentricities, not to call it by a harder word, by this time. Of course it's very wrong and improper and all that, but still, − " "My dear Clara, say imprudent, which is worse than any amount of immorality. Un péché caché est à moitié pardonné,[1] and I don't see the smallest chance of her fault being hidden, if she behaves in this absurd manner every night." "Exactly. Every night she does, and I don't suppose there's any more danger this particular one than any other." "Logically reasoned, I suppose, no. But we cannot account for impressions and I have a foreboding of coming evil I cannot shake off tonight." "O Alice don't!" and Clara gave a shiver of horror that brought all the hair she had carefully been pinning up, tumbling down her shoulders again. "I have great faith in presentiments, and would give £5 to see May safely back in her room again. What on earth shall we do!" "Nothing!" I answered, getting up and taking my candle, "seeing neither of us, I should think, intend losing our characters by invading Mr Ogle's room too. Goodnight, darling. Let events take their course, which perhaps will be as smooth as usual − don't excite yourself into a nightmare on the subject."

Still, notwithstanding these reassuring words, I felt far from easy and once in my room, took up a book, instead of going to bed as usual. I read for about half an hour, and had just begun to forget May, and grow sleepy over my heroine's fictitious sorrows, when a tremendous row just over me, as of some hard substance knocking against a wall (I learnt next day it was Johnny Ogle's head) and a woman's voice shrill and frightened, convinced me my fears had not been unfounded, and that the storm had broke. Throwing on a dressing gown, I jumped up, opened the door, and after these preparations, devoted all my ears and intelligence to hear all that was going on. "Alice," came at last in the most subdued tone from the other side of the passage, and on answering in another moment Clara was in my arms, clinging to me for protection, and sobbing as if she were the guilty and discovered heroine of this unpleasant adventure. I dosed her with eau de cologne, scolded her a little for this exhibition of terror, and sent her back to her room, to despatch her husband upstairs to watch the progress of events, reassured. Next day, and what an unpleasant day it was! we

---

[1]"Un péché caché est à moitié pardonné" − A sin concealed is half pardoned.

had all the details. It appears Manners, wishing to speak to May that particularly awkward evening, took the liberty of going into her room uninvited. There were her bracelets, necklace, even the dress she had worn, but no sign of the lady herself. "Where's your mistress?" he asked sharply enough of the soubrette in waiting, and that astute damsel, without raising her eyes from the jewels she was putting away, answered demurely "Gone to wish Miss Edith goodnight." The excuse was a sufficiently plausible one; unhappily, unbelieving Manners, marvelling much at this access of maternal devotion from careless May, took it into his head to pay his little daughter a visit also, and verify the exactitude of his information. Edith, he found: but needless to say, not a sign of the delinquent. And then: — how the idea occurred to him, I don't know how, unless provoked by that unhappy destiny which is always meddling with everything that least concerns it — Manners directed his steps towards the gentlemen's bedrooms, and meeting Mr Ogle, peering about the corridor, with a persistency that looked very like reconnoitering if the coast were clear, passed his arm familiarly within his enemy's and led him back to his, Johnny Ogle's room, where May was standing, calmly awaiting her lover's return. — Tableau!!

* * * * *

The scene that ensued, I have already partly described; poor Manners' gentlemanly disregard of his wife's conduct, I am sorry to say, failed him: the elasticity of his conjugal principles subjected to so severe a stretch gave way under the ordeal. Forgetting all his aristocratic indifference he threw himself upon Mr Ogle, and gave that young gentleman's head some of those sound raps against the wall that I had heard, and should be glad to see distributed to every mauvais sujet caught under the same circumstances. Unfortunately the noise brought Father and more of the gentlemen to the spot. My old Boy rescued Johnny Ogle whose head was fast assuming the appearance of a pancake, and hurried May downstairs followed by some remarks more truthful than pleasant in their tenor.

And — as in the midst of every tragedy there is generally a comic element — Mr Ogle turned to Colonel Verschoyle with a piteous face to enquire if his personal beauty had been damaged in the struggle, on which the other led him to a glass, that he might contemplate at his ease the uncompromising black eye with which the irate husband had gratified him.

At daybreak he left, telling the servants important business called him to London: and so we may dismiss him from these pages with the sincere wish every other offender in the same line may be brought to a similar confusion!

Amen, So be it.

*　*　*　*　*

I wouldn't have been Clara today for any consideration: for on her fell the onerous task of comforting afflicted May, who wept the whole day, like all the bereaved mothers of Israel put together, over the loss of her last plaything and bemoaned Manners' brutality in the most piteous terms. Poor Manners! Why *I* viewing his conduct from the height of my hard-heartedness, look upon it as a model of marital consideration and — if the truth must out — imbecility; an idea entirely shared by all the gentlemen. One goodlooking young Guardsman gave as his opinion to the others "What is the good of all you fellows going on making such a fuss and using such high-sounding terms of condemnation? It's over now, and the only thing remaining, is for Mrs Manners Sutton to dry her tears, and elect Johnny's successor. 'Le roi est mort, vive le roi.' My boys, let's go in and win!" at which the others laughed and fully agreed with him.

Meanwhile, with a despairing countenance, Clara came in search of me. "I can't do anything with May," she declared, letting herself fall wearily into an armchair, "she does nothing but cry and exclaim about her darling Johnny. I am sick of hearing the man's name and tired of playing sympathy. It would be only Christian charity on your part to come and relieve me a little" — a suggestion I acted upon, only so far from sympathising I gave May such a bit of my mind and in such plain terms, that though she began by abusing me, calling me cruel and crying worse than ever, she finished by drying her tears and listening in mute admiration, while I declaimed much as follows — "Really to hear you my dear child, one would think there wasn't another man to be found in the world, instead of there being hundreds infinitely superior in every way to your lost sheep, ready and willing to supply his deficiency. And now that he is gone you may let me wonder what on earth you could ever have seen in him! Besides, even supposing him invested with all the graces I conclude your imagination adorned him with, a species of moustached Apollo exquisitely turned out by Poole,[1] a model to the jeunesse dorée of the 19th

[1] A Savile Row tailor.

century, even then, and how different he is to the picture I have drawn you cannot but own, he would not be worth a quarter of the tears you've been shedding on his behalf — Clara! I appeal to you: did you ever, I won't say meet, that would be expecting too much, but even hear of the man worth spoiling your eyes and appearance for: which undesirable result, my dear May, allow me to inform you, your present conduct is rapidly achieving." Of course Clara supported me, though she hadn't the moral courage to point out these home truths herself, declaring such a phoenix[1] never existed. May, touched in her feminine vanity, after a long scrutiny of the pretty face disfigured with tears her glass reflected, began to agree with us; besides what a woman really appreciates in her lover, is not the feelings he excites in her own breast, but the regard in which her friends hold him, therefore seeing how disparagingly we both spoke of her choice, she began to conclude there must be something radically wrong with it: from which sentiment to a sense of relief that this esclandre had at least put an end to the liaison, only a step is wanting. "Still!" she exclaimed, turning from examining her face to fire this parting shot, "Though you don't think Johnny was worth wasting my time on, you must own, Alice, that Manners made a great fool of himself. Really to have heard the row and confusion he made, one would think it was the first time such a thing had occurred to me." Which naïf remark sent both Clara and me into fits of laughter, in which this unhappy victim of a husband's brutality could not refrain from joining: — and so peace was partially restored.

* * * * *

All these startling events had quite put Sir John and his attentions out of my mind; not so with him, however, and as he is to go early tomorrow, he resolved to bring matters to a crisis this evening. As ill luck would have it, he caught me by myself in the cedar room, standing with my head leaning against the mantel piece, looking down idly into the fire, my thoughts as far from him as from Kelham itself. Not being gifted however with second sight, he may be excused from not divining it and of course my good breeding was sufficient to conceal any open expression of annoyance at his intrusion. He joined me then, and after a few banal remarks, during which I was meditating a plausible excuse for disappearing, began lamenting his

[1]Perhaps Alice meant "paragon"?

solitude, in a sentimental tone, that my quick perceptions caught, and thought boded no good. "I can't say I pity you in the least," was my slightly heartless answer, to some touching tirade on his loneliness and desolation, "you are your own master, and if the country bores you, which I don't the least wonder at, take a house in London and patronise the Park morning and afternoon. You'll find plenty of society there." And moving a step or two back, for he was getting unpleasantly near, I looked straight into the fire as if it was the only object the least worthy of exciting my attention. But all this little manège was, I am sorry to say, entirely thrown away on the individual for whose edification it was enacted. When a man has once made up his mind to make a fool of himself it requires nothing less than an earthquake to stop him: hints, innuendoes and such slight arrows glancing back harmless from the impenetrable armour of masculine imbecility: − Sir John advanced the two steps I had gone back, seized both my hands and held them pretty tightly: a manoeuvre that took me utterly unawares but which I strongly resented. But I might as well have struggled with a band of iron, I only hurt myself by running the bracelet I wore into my arm. Therefore, reflecting that after all, if it gave him any particular pleasure I ought to be too charitable to mind, I desisted, and listened patiently enough, to what he was saying. "Dull! It isn't that the country bores me, any more than London would. On the contrary I used to live there most peacefully, content with my books and my horses for all companionship: and I was cheerful and happy until I met you!" Here he paused; carried my captive hands passionately to his lips, and drew me towards him, evidently with the intention of inflicting quite a different caress, but I was too quick for him, it would take a startling event indeed to take me thus at fault, snatching my hands away, I pushed him back with more strength and goodwill than he probably gave me credit for, exclaiming indignantly "I think you are forgetting yourself, Sir John, and if for one moment you imagine you can behave to me in the same way as to Mrs Manners Sutton, you had better undeceive yourself!!" to which he responded more earnestly than before "You are quite wrong, and it is very unjust of you to attribute any such ideas to me, when my dearest wish is that you would give me a right to love and cherish you, to call you by the sweet and sacred name of −" "Alice! May wants to speak to you − I've been looking for you everywhere!" − the opportune disturbance came from Father, and you may guess how willingly I obeyed the summons, whispering to Sir John as I passed

"Let our conversation cease here, for nothing of the sort could ever be!" and my tone was so resolute that, for a wonder, he believed me, and accepted his dismissal as irrevocable — coming down at my usual late hour next morning, I was informed he had left for Scotland — a pleasant journey to him — and good sport!

* * * * *

This little episode terminated my visit. Clara left early this morning Tuesday September 22nd and lamented, pretty little hypocrite! over the parting just as if she felt really sorry. After all, we got a certain amount of pleasure out of each other's society, as for Father, he's as devoted to her as her husband is to me. In fact she began with the remark after a minute's reflection "Miss Miles, I don't like you half so well as your Father!" to which I replied, "Mrs Verschoyle, I don't like you half as well as your husband: which curious fact may be explained by the natural aversion women always seem to entertain towards each other and the still more decided preference they habitually evince towards mankind!" — which home thrust I firmly believe obtained me the little lady's good graces for the nonce: though I can't say I quite believe in her patte de velours, even now; I'm sure she did say something nasty to my retriever, or he wouldn't always have been warning me against her. To come back to today, we left at eleven-thirty: and had the chance of meeting Mr Harry Fane at the station. We travelled some way together, and he promised me a pho of his goodlooking face, which I shall believe in when I see it.

> The new art of photography intrigued everyone greatly and there seems to have been much exchanging of portraits among friends and acquaintances; having someone's "pho" in your possession did not necessarily imply any emotional involvement with the subject. There was a craze as early as the 1850s for printing such portraits the size of visiting cards, and these *cartes de visite* pictures were freely exchanged.

The Doldrums

LICE left Kelham to return to her grandfather's establishment at Leigh Court, Somerset. This architecturally astonishing place has a history similar to that of many a "gentleman's seat". Founded as a monastery in 1143, it was passed at the Dissolution in 1536 to Henry VIII's new Bishop of Bristol, Paul Bush, and on his death to Sir George Norton. Norton built a Tudor mansion which was demolished in 1811, to make way for the "modern" Leigh Court built in 1814 from designs by Thomas Hopper. Its owner, Philip Miles, was the son of the William Miles who made his fortune in Jamaica.

No expense was spared and no luxury denied. A writer of the last century says:

About one mile from Rownham ferry, a bold and handsome Ionic gateway and lodge form the entrance into the demesne. On entering the inner park the scenery is luxuriant and the prospects delightfully varied. On the right is a deep and well-wooded glen

. . . with occasional views of the Avon. Immediately around the house is a thriving plantation of evergreens, intermingled with trees of great size and beauty, some of which overhang a narrow romantic glen which separates the pleasure grounds and lawn from the park, to which the deer are confined by an iron fence scarcely perceptible. The south, as the principal entrance, has an Ionic portico, supported by four massive columns . . . The mansion is surrounded by an extensive lawn, bounded by shrubberies, intersected by winding footpaths. The principal apartments are a vestibule on the south side; on the left a billiard-room and study; on the opposite side a music room which leads to the library . . . The entrance from the portico on the south side opens into a vestibule, which is enclosed by a circle of light marble columns with Ionic capitals. The floor is formed of alternate radiating circles of black and white marble, and opens into the great hall. This apartment possesses singular architectural beauty, and attracts universal admiration. A double flight of steps leads to a peristyle of the Ionic order, around which are twenty appropriate columns supporting a lofty dome lighted by painted glass, and adorned with highly enriched panels. The floor is of chequered marble . . .[1]

A twentieth-century description goes on: the morning room "has a delicate Adam ceiling, retaining traces of original colour. To the north is the library, fifty feet long and half as wide. It has a deeply coffered ceiling and was once lined with handsome bookcases . . . The original mauve fireplaces are missing." The drawing room "is the grandest of the rooms. It is extravagantly decorated in the most elaborate Adam manner, in red and green and gold. The ceiling and door and window cases are heavily encrusted with applied pre-cast anthemion and other mouldings . . ." The saloon ceiling "has a circular radiating pattern and the original gilt-brass lantern hangs from its centre. The floor is entirely covered with inlaid woods. Black geometrical patterns are worked in large squares on a background of honey-coloured oak . . . All these rooms still have their fine mahogany double doors, some of which retain original gilt brass handles, with pierced back-plates . . . The public rooms enjoy views of the park . . . In addition to the eight great rooms on the ground floor there were fourteen principal

[1]*West Country Houses* by Robert V. Cooke, published by the author, 1957.

bedrooms on the first floor."[1] And there were twenty-two servants' rooms, and stabling for thirty horses.

But although in the 1860s the house was in its prime, to Alice the "prospects" were *not* "delightfully varied". She anticipated little joy from a sojourn under the régime of her grandparents, and the one bright spot was the visit she expected from Lord Petersham. On September 22nd she records receiving confirmation of this — though it was hardly exhilarating: "Arrived at Leigh I found a letter from Lord Petersham awaiting me saying that as he might not come till the 28th, he could only stay till the 30th; still that was . . ."

At this interesting point Alice has cut four pages out of her notebook. One half-sentence remains: ". . . laughed as if I had never been so merry in my life . . ." Was it humiliation, rage or simply bitter disappointment she was trying to wipe out when she excised those pages? All we can be sure of is that her grandmother prevented Lord Petersham's visit, as may be seen from the next entry on September 29th, and from other references later in the diary.

Why Lady Miles should have done this we cannot know, but it is impossible to resist speculation. Did she have something against the young man, or was she shocked by her daughter-in-law's blatant husband-hunting on Alice's behalf? It seems unlikely that Alice would have felt compelled to destroy evidence concerning Lord Petersham's credentials: either she would have been persuaded by her grandmother's arguments or — more likely — she would vigorously have protested against them. But if what happened stemmed from her grandmother's opinion of her mother's moral character, nerves would have been exposed.

We have her statement that there had been more than one "stand-up fight" between her mother and her grandmother before the invitation was sent, which had made her want "to escape from my own thoughts and all these worries"; we have her comment "at least so she says" when her mother goes to stay with a friend at Budleigh Salterton (see page 50). We will soon hear of a hideous row at Leigh Court "of a species I don't care to report even here". We know that her grandparents were very respectable and religious and we know that her mother was not: indeed, before Alice's story is done we will have

[1]Ibid.

learnt a good deal about Mrs Miles's carryings-on and the extent to which Alice was sometimes, in spite of her closeness to her mother, upset by them. So if Alice's grandmother was disgusted — as many high-minded Victorian gentlewomen would have been — by Mrs Miles's worldly insistence on chasing a young nobleman whom she hardly knew in the vulgar hope of Alice's "catching" him, the resulting battle may have brought many disagreeable matters out from under stones, making the whole drama even more disturbing, and therefore worthy of suppression, than the loss of Lord Petersham in itself.

Tuesday September 29th

Minnie[1] came home last night, and I went and lunched with her today. I don't know that there is any inordinate affection existing between us, but my nerves have been so completely unstrung with all these rows, that I regularly clung to her when we met; and kissed her in that passionate way that coming from one woman to another, may be taken as an infallible sign, that a man is at the bottom of the emotion. I told her my troubles and we both indulged in a thorough abuse of Grandmamma, the mutual dislike we bear her being our strong point of sympathy.

I wonder if in another world I shall discover of what use one's relations were to one, for I don't see the faintest likelihood of my solving the mystery in this. I labour at present under the idea that they are a species of penance imposed upon us by a far-seeing Providence, to punish us for all the misdeeds of our life, past, present and to come. Certainly if this be really the case they carry out the rôle imposed upon them most admirably: see their present conduct for proof. Yes, depend upon it the cattle [?] ought to be suppressed, and if only they would bring a bill to that effect into the House of Lords instead of fighting about that stupid "Irish Church" no one cares for, I'm sure it would pass without the slightest opposition and our future life would be greatly benefited by the change. But though abusing them is a slight relief to my mind and therefore I indulge in it; — I am sorry to

[1]Probably the Minnie Vaughn who reappears later and seems to be a cousin.

say it does not in the least hurt them, or remedy the hopeless existing state of affairs. Oh —— ! I shall probably never see you again now! and I had been looking forward to this meeting more than words can say. When I think of it I could sit down and cry myself into a hopeless state of imbecility; if it were not for the reflection that such a proceeding would materially damage my personal appearance; and thus preclude any chance of finding consolation elsewhere.

I stayed till quite late with Minnie, and on leaving found Edie waiting to walk home with me. I have not had much need to mention my sisters: this my particular favourite is as pretty and intelligent a girl of fourteen, as it would be possible to discover, and perfectly devoted to me, ce qui ne gâte rien[1]. There's another row progressing at the Court, she declares, and very properly she had walked up to warn me. Mon Dieu! Mon Dieu! what can be up now! Since I have no visit to expect no words can express how thankful I shall be to get away from this hotbed of iniquity.

* * * * *

More trouble? I should rather think there was: and heaven alone knows what may come of it — of a species too, I don't care to record even here, but one good at least comes out of all this evil, we leave on Thursday, and having once escaped it will be a very long time before homesickness overcomes me sufficiently, to make me put my feet within the doors here, during my grandmother's reign, and as, like good, evil is eternal, I expect she'll last a good time yet.

Thursday October 1st

Of course I had to write and tell my retriever he couldn't come to Mr Savile's, seeing as bad luck would have it, it's today we leave, still par hasard[2] I mentioned our train and its destination. Started with the most gloomy anticipation concerning our comfort en route, owing to Mother's threat of taking the baby[3] with us first class, and after a slight upset on the road, arrived to have them agreeably dispersed; for contrary to her usual habits, that fickle Goddess Fortune had for once thought fit to make a slight deviation from her general rule, in our favour, and came to the assistance of the oppressed and innocent. While I was on the qui vive for a Taunton train, up steamed our own,

[1]"ce qui ne gâte rien" — which does no harm.
[2]"Par hasard" — by chance, or "I just happened to mention . . ."
[3]Violet Bessie, who was to die in 1883 at the age of sixteen.

and the first person who got out of it was Moreland Hutton.

Of course he changed into our carriage, the objectionable baby was banished, and under these happy auspices we started.

I looked upon this charming rencontre in spite of all adverse circumstances, as a decided victory over the Philistines, and diligently endeavoured to follow the advice of a clergyman I heard the other day, who informed us we should always make the most of the opportunities Providence is mercifully pleased to vouchsafe us: looking back I think I may say I conscientiously fulfilled my duty in that respect today. He has been staying with Lord Kensington, to whom he declared he had important business in Bristol, to account for his leaving by that early and inconvenient train: my good doggie! he really appeared unfeignedly glad to see me again: more so indeed than that uncompromising mother of his would probably have approved of. We discussed Kelham a good deal of course, and I gave him an account of the late disturbances that lost nothing in the telling. How he did laugh to be sure, when I wound up by recounting May's naïf remark "Really to hear the row John makes, one would think it was the first time such a thing had occurred to me." Then he attacked me about Col. Eyre, on the strength of those most improper verses on my "jolie bouche", which it appears he sent Moreland who pretended to believe that I'd flirted with him, an accusation most indignantly repudiated. "Just fancy me wasting my time on a married man, and such a married man too! when tall slight individuals are my particular weakness!" which remark my vain retriever chose to apply to himself after begging pardon and abandoning his utterly unfounded statements which to use his own expression, he'd only adopted "to get a rise out of me". — It was my turn to attack now, so I put him through a cross examination respecting his own misdemeanours in general and those relating to Lady D in particular, which Sir John had been sufficiently amiable to inform me of. As far as I can make out, all the advances came from her, though of course he was too gentlemanly to say so: anyhow he never goes near them now, et elle est fort laide ce qui l'essentiel![1]

Just before leaving little Tommy Bowles rose out of his insignificance and covered himself with glory by making verses on Kelham and its proceedings. These lines, as good luck would have it, I had in my pocket and produced for my retriever's benefit: he copied out these verses —

[1]et elle est . . . and she's very ugly, which is crucial.

There was pearly Alice Miles
A clear-cut gem-like face
That's perfect mistress of the wiles
By which men fall from grace.
You'll not approach her if you're wise
Unless she welcomes you:
If in her eyes, salvation lies
Perdition lies there too.

(This Moreland was audacious enough to think a most perfect
description, mais passons!)

That pretty man Sir Arundel
Was rather neat than Neave
Salt tears from lovely Cator fell
That he so soon should leave.
But Sister Anne, what did you see
When you and Cator drew
Each tower and tree so earnestly
From any point of view?

There's Wombwell whom the parrot loves
Verschoyle the genial cynic
And Eyre who when he dances moves
Light as his patronymic.
And sweet Sir John who goes the way
Of lucky Moreland Hutton
For whom one day, fair Alice may
Have cared — well — just one button.

(This is all he copied, but I think this verse rather good also —)

Gentle Johnny leads the way
And by all mortals quoted
To be in this dull present day
Of lovers most devoted.
Were Venus prize at whom Jove nods
Did all Olympians want her
Against the Gods, I'll lay all odds
And win her in a canter.

There's handsome bearded Philip Miles
And darling Mr Denison
To whom at Doncaster with smiles
The ladies gave their benison.

He needed it, for Yorkshire's fair
Kicked up an awful row
Because they could not theirs compare
With Kelham beauty show.

One memory too we all shall trace
When the full page is read
His courteous grave and manly face
Who graces the table's head.
Well, I shall wish full many a day
That Kelham's towers were near
And that I may be toujours prêt
Pour bien y parvenir.[1]

On my naturally mentioning Mrs Verschoyle's name Moreland began warning me about her again and after a great amount of coaxing persuasion he at last owned that she had said lots of disagreeable things to him about me such as "Pretty? oh yes, Alice is pretty enough in all conscience: happily for her, seeing she will bring nothing but her bright eyes to her husband in marriage." Then she assured him I had said "A cold unimpressionable man, Mr Hutton, is he? a disbeliever in the efficacy of women's charms. Well, I bet you a pair of gloves, best kid four buttons, that before he leaves I will have brought him into the most abject state of submission." Of course I indignantly denied having ever said anything of the sort, and of course he implicitly believed me: Really Clara is a great idiot, that she has come to the age of thirty-two without finding out the most infallible method of making an enemy even of your greatest friend is to tell him any harm about the woman he has taken a fancy to, more especially if you prove it. He's a curious young man too, is my retriever: only fancy his having written to Col. Eyre to find out when we should be at Leigh etc., instead of asking himself. Then he alluded to our last scene in the cedar room, that I for my part had almost forgotten. "Do you remember that thick gold bracelet of yours falling off, and my picking it up and clasping it for you? You were kneeling on the hearth rug warming yourself, and as I stooped over your arm to arrange the ornament, you can have no idea how tempting the sweet face looked,

---

[1]toujours prêt . . . And that I may always be ready to get there. The family's motto was "Pour y parvenir, toujour prêt" – "Always ready to achieve".

turned to mine in the firelight. Looking back I wonder how my self-possession ever carried me through such an ordeal; it was happy that it did though, for little Edith owned afterwards she'd been watching us all the time through the window." "If that's her usual habit, I should think she saw very strange things sometimes" I said laughing, and then he went on to tell me the sort of reputation Kelham bears in the county, as being a house no woman under forty should venture into, adding he sincerely hoped never to see me there again, which he probably never will. Poor Kelham! Its morals were certainly d'occasion but still it didn't strike me as being as bad as all that. Then Moreland went on to tell me of his home, and Justin [?][1] his youngest brother who seems to be most shamefully spoiled by the whole family. He is in some crack regiment of cavalry, while poor Moreland went through the Crimean campaign, and a year's knocking about in India in a hundred and something or other infantry corps. Of course he interspersed his conversation with several of those pretty little no-things that coming from a man of his stamp mean so much, to all of which I listened with downcast eyes, smiling mouth, and the general air of soft contentment you may remark on the countenance of a cat when she is being petted. The train meanwhile rushed along with the most unnecessary speed, and was in London before we thought we were halfway. He stayed till the very last, only leaving us at the Paddington Hotel, and I declare I could have cried with vexation when we said goodbye. Alas! alas! with my last glimpse of his handsome face, fades away my last english flirtation, and I may make up my mind now to Paris and those insupportable frenchmen for the next six months, to say nothing of an indefinite period beyond!

[1]The name looks like Justin in Alice's hand, but *Burke's Landed Gentry* of 1863 gives the younger brother as Edmund. He was a Cornet in the Royal Dragoons.

Discontent
and Diversions

LICE'S gloom at returning to France was miti-
gated by a new acquaintance of her father's, a Mr
Hamilton Becket (or Beckett) whom she nicknamed the Cardinal (perhaps mistakenly supposing
that Thomas à Becket had been one). He was
introduced as "a very rich and goodlooking young
widower" so she pounced on him as "a profitable
opening for my abilities". Unfortunately he turned
out to be not widowed but merely separated, so less
"profitable" than she had hoped. But she decided
that he was old enough to look after himself, so if
he insisted on heaping her with roses and marrons glacés, and taking
her and her mother to the theatre in the most expensive loges, why
should she deny him the pleasure?

This helped her to get through October and November cheerfully enough; and for December she was offered what she expected to be "another world to study and subdue". A Colonel Mountjoy Martyn, who lived near Ipswich, spent a month in Paris, fell in love with Alice's mother, and ended by inviting first the Dear Boy, then Mrs Miles and Alice, to stay at his home, Broke Hall.

Alas, the party assembled there turned out to be one of "patriarchs" – old old men in their fifties and sixties, "the one redeeming feature" being a forty-four-year-old widower with whom she was able to enter into "the tiniest little passage of arms" in the rare moments when the gentlemen were not out shooting, or in the smoking room digesting the curries which "Col. Martyn has an Egyptian down from London to make". Luckily the Colonel had a fifteen-year-old daughter called Jeanne, a lively and impressionable girl with whom Alice became great friends.

It was to Jeanne that Alice told a story (later written into her diary in *Schrift*) about a Frenchman whom she detested. It is not immediately clear why she used her code for it, since her virtue is not compromised. The man became too pressing, she spurned him, and in revenge he told her mother that Alice had tried to seduce him. Having created an atmosphere of suspense, passion and betrayal, the story peters out with Alice in disgrace with her mother, who favours the young man's interpretation of the event. The real significance of the tale, and the reason for disguising it in *Schrift*, seems to be that the young man, Louis Fieron (nicknamed Tartuffe after Molière's hypocrite), was Mrs Miles's admirer. Some of Alice's later references to him hint at something more and make it clear that she was made extremely uncomfortable by her mother's weakness for Tartuffe, but she never goes so far as to give an exact reason for her uneasiness and disapproval.

Sunday 3rd January 1869

Went to church devoutly, and heard the most excellent discourse from the Rev Edward Forbes, but so full of applications for grace and patience and the Holy Spirit and other celestial things to the utter exclusion of earthly needs, that I felt almost inclined to cry out — "Dear Lord, I don't want all that — only give me ——!" Wasn't it wicked? Mais voilà, c'etait ma façon de penser[1], and I record it accordingly.

Copy of a letter to Jeanne, undated

Tuesday 4th January was the first Tuileries ball, and if you got the Evening Star of the 5th you will have seen a full account of my dress and general appearance. In case you did not, I copy out the bit referring to us: — "Miss Miles was à la Watteau, a demi-traine of white satin falling from the shoulders, the rest of her graceful costume also white, and her only ornament a ribbon of blue velvet, perdu among her golden curls. 'La Poesie en personne' remarked Mme du Caze, and as women rarely bestow praise on each other, I record this heroic outburst of generous feeling."

Isn't that rather complimentary? I only hope a good angel will throw it in the way of some friends of mine who shall be nameless, and who would I think fully appreciate it. And now for détails intimes. The Ball wasn't very amusing, no ball in Paris to my mind ever is: though the floors were polished to a stage of ideal perfection only to be attained in this capital; the orchestre conducted by Strauss, the supper pronounced unexceptional, and last but not least, my toilette and general appearance the envy of every feminine beholder. What more could the most exacting individual require? Et voilà! Solve the mystery as you choose, but certain it is that in the midst of a dance with one of my chief admirers, I caught myself stifling a lady-like little yawn; a yawn that, waiting for Mars and bored by Vulcan, Venus herself might, without any injury to her appearance have indulged in: — and wished very sincerely indeed, that I was cozily curled up in my bed, and asleep, at home, instead of performing fantastic steps dignified by the name of polka mazurka, under the eyes of the Emperor, Empress, assembled court, and some 15,000 spectators. What a model little wife I shall be some day, to be sure, Jeanne, when I can make up my mind to undergo the ordeal of matrimony, and exchange my liberty (such as it is!) for one master instead of two, and diamond-rivetted fetters. I am sure under such circumstances I should not care one bit about going out, and as for dancing! is it not even now, my pet abomination? I often feel inclined to try the "Ladies

[1]c'etait ma façon de penser: it was the way I thought.

Committee District Visitation" dissipation; it couldn't be more utter vanity and vexation of spirit than the treadmill of society we dignify by the appellation "amusement" and season after season toil so laboriously through. Distributing broth, flannel petticoats and good advice to the poorer brethren would, I daresay, if one had sufficient strength of mind to try it, be to the full as pleasant and much more profitable, than sitting listening to inane compliments heard a hundred times before: and after a certain amount of practice in well-doing I daresay one would manage to get up as lively an interest in the spiritual welfare of a plain-headed but otherwise eminently worthy ploughman as we do at present in the misdeeds of a goodlooking blasé young guardsman. Anyhow, the experiment would be worth trying if only for its novelty.

> Alice's comments on this ball are confirmed by *Vanity Fair*, January 7th 1869. The weekly Letter from Paris reported as follows: "Madame and Mademoiselle Miles, two of your compatriots, made a sensation, less by their dresses than by their beauty. Madame Miles looked so young that she might have been her daughter's elder sister." (This was in French — the magazine was able to take for granted that its readers would understand it.) A new and surprising tone appears in Alice's next entry.

What I did not write to Jeanne as I don't think she'd either appreciate or understand it, was the half hour's unalloyed happiness I enjoyed last Sunday, at the Rue d'Aguesseau church where I have gone through so many hours utter ennui. Mr Cox who I met at the Stainforths had indeed prepared my mind for something out of the common in Mr Pichoux[?]'s preaching. I went prepared to criticise [not] expecting much, and left enchanted, still under the spell of an eloquence I never heard equalled. I don't pose for goodness, heaven knows, and my book will testify, that I have no small quantity on my conscience of those venial sins pretty women indulge in: still listening to Mr P [?] today I felt — no, I can't describe it! something better in me struggling to the surface, some of the intense besoin d'aimer suffocating me, though always put down, always repressed, manifesting itself in all its power and exclaiming "at last there is something I can love, an affection I can cling to and that will satisfy my infinite craving after tenderness. Oh if this merciful heaven would only take me to itself, now, at once, and hide me away from all the bitter trials or passive misery of this life. This life, that at eighteen, I am so tired, so unutterably wearied of. Yes, let me die, a peaceful painless death, let me lie under some grassy mound, in the churchyard[1] where I dreamt such sweet dreams never to be realised, and which is dearer to me than almost any other spot on earth; let me lie there, unconscious, forgotten, and be at rest for ever. An object of complete indifference to my parents, I have nothing to keep me in this world where no one would miss me. No baby's clinging fingers, no husband's detaining arms and fond caresses, therefore let me go, to this bright heaven, so beautifully described. I must have something to love me, I must, I must! And so I wish Jesus would take me to another world and give me what I cannot find in this". For the hundredth time all these bitter thoughts passed through my mind, whilst I sat with bowed head and clasped hands, listening to the beautiful sermon till at last — how soon it seemed — the clergyman stopped speaking, the solemn blessing was given, and once outside the church door Mother startled me out of myself by exclaiming "Look at that awkward man, he nearly tore my dress!" the petty cares of life came trooping back again, and the spell was broken. Oh, ——, ——, if only I had you to help me!

Saturday 6 February

I am better, much better, though still in bed, for since my last entry a fluxion de poitrine[2] has laid me on the broad of my back and treated me to a fortnight's inaction, submitted to with the most perfect philosophy, which ought to have been highly gratifying to my physician, instead of which Dr Bavereau does his best to rouse me, and persists in considering this indifference as a bad sign. Try and please the Faculty again after such a flagrant case as this! and you fully deserve the failure certain to attend your efforts. Mrs N Peat paid me a visit today "You've been very bad, poor child," she said with a sympathy none the less gratifying that I didn't feel the least entitled to it, "in fact a week ago the Dr almost despaired of saving you!" "I wish he hadn't troubled himself" was my somewhat ungracious reply, "you can't think, dear, when I was at my worst, the temptation came over me to get up, open the window, and breathe

---

[1]Could the "churchyard" have been that at Kelham, where she dallied briefly with Morland Hutton?
[2]Inflammation of the lungs.

several mouthfuls of the frosty air, which would have finished me, for which no one's sorrow would have equalled my joy." — which remark drew down on me a shower of abuse and remonstrance: it's quite true though, when I find something worth living for I will wish to live — until then! — on me passera mes opinions[1].

I have had 2 or 3 letters from little Sydney Gladstone, the youngest, humblest and probably the most in earnest of all my adorers. I made the poor boy's conquest most involuntarily, one evening at the North Peats, just before leaving for London, and on my return receiving such an account of the state of his affections from Madame —— also being most merciful when mercy costs me nothing, hit on the brilliant idea of writing and telling him to collect army monograms for me, that being the newest diversion prevalent in the grand monde for losing time. My laziness has always prevented me falling a victim to this mania, nothing being more wearisome in my opinion than a constant hunt for little bits of paper, and general worriting of all your acquaintances, necessary to get a really good collection, and yet thanks to Sydney, I have such a one now in my possession as would make the amateurs of such-like bêtises turn green with envy: with such little discrimination does Fortune shower her gifts: it's no question of being worthy, the only thing requisite when the generous mood seizes the goddess is to be in the way.

* * * * *

What bores me a good deal, is that Mother's head, always fruitful in ideas, has just furnished her with a new one, most objectionable in its tendency. Being unable to put down my weariness of life, myself, society and the world to its real reason, she has forged one for herself, and chooses to imagine, upheld by the Dr who my indifference puzzles, that I'm in love. Then unhappily, during the fever that used to seize me every night, and once under the influence of a strong narcotic, a name, the name that is always in my thoughts, came too often to my lips in accents that grew tender when they murmured it. To him I appealed constantly, for pity, for protection, in imaginary dangers delirium evoked, and she was there hearing all, which is little calculated to make her alter her opinions. A pleasant time I shall have of it I expect, at my recovery. Oh, if only we could go and live in London, but Father writes that the houses are quite beyond his

[1]Forgive my opinions.

means, and I may resign myself to remain where I am. The best years
of my life, and to lose them so utterly, dans un intérieur que je déteste,
et un pays que j'abhorre.[1] Besides every day, struggle as I may, I feel
myself growing worse and worse, nay losing almost the hatred and
loathing of sin, getting accustomed to it in fact, than the which
nothing can be more fatal, in this uncongenial atmosphere. And I
could be so different; I feel it, God knows it. If only he would give me
the means and position, the good I would do, the tears I would dry,
the suffering my ready hand should appease, and the happiness I
should find in doing it. Then my home, for after all that is the first
consideration, besides which the others fade into nothing, how bright
it should be, how my husband should respect as well as love me. Wife
and mother, sacred names, the only ones really worth living for, when
kept unstained, higher titles for a woman than Queen or Princess. I
have been fairest among the fair, spoiled and smiled on for my beauty,
for two seasons now. Sweetest incense to a woman, they say, but the
idea's a fallacy. I've found out the vanity and weariness of it all,
understand its hollowness and insincerity at eighteen. If God ever
sends me the happy life I dream, and later on a little daughter to nestle
in my bosom and be all my own — my darling, my darling, how I will
love you, and guard you, and shield you from this world — what a
different mother I will be to you, to what mine has been to me.

Monday 11 February

Dear Boy came back from Broke where he has been spending the past
fortnight, bringing me a chatty pleasant enough letter from Jeanne,
and the invigorating intelligence that in the whole of London he could
not find a house to suit him, so I might make up my mind to remain
where we are. He consents, however, to go and spend the season
there, and d'ici là, who knows what may happen! Jeanne says "I was
asked the other day if you were the Alice Miles Lansdowne was in love
with. Having that piece of information, you ought to play your cards
well and carefully, and who knows but what you may yet be the
mistress of the mansion in Berkeley Square." I like the way she
suggests that last idea; for all the world comme s'il ne s'agissait que de
vouloir[2]. No, indeed, his Lordship is not at all the sort of young man

[1]In a household which I detest and a country which I abhor.
[2]As if it were just a matter of wishing.

to be captured merely by my esprit and joli minois chiffonné![1] valuable as both articles undoubtedly are. I came to that conclusion long ago: and if I continued a certain demure little flirtation with him, it was merely from force of habit, and the reflexion he may be useful in introducing someone else. It's a pity too, for with my ambitions to back his own abilities, le garçon là ira loin[2]. I studied him closely during the fortnight he was in Paris, beginning at his pretty hands and feet a lady might be proud of and ending with his keen grey eyes, that have so little weakness about them: and came to the conclusion, after due consideration of the subject, that he would be very lovable indeed, if − he were not a marquis and owner of £70,000 a year. For as to being in love with a man in that position, you might as well talk of the tender passion in conjunction with Napoleon III, and how Mme de Castiglione and the rest of his favourites would laugh, to be sure, if accused of such an enormity.

*   *   *   *   *

There is a legend here, almost too absurd to mention, and yet generally credited, that if you give something to the first beggar of the male sex who applies to you for assistance on New Year's Day, one of his names will bear the same initial as the husband Fate reserves you. "Louis Berthold" a pretty curly-haired gamin enough, was the first that came across my path January 1869. I wrote his name down carefully with a laugh at the superstition: Jeanne doubtless would back up her suggestion if only she knew. Pour moi I can only say I sincerely hope there is no foreshadowing of coming events in it, it being clearly against ——— . Oh dear! My favourite Pascal says, that a beggar who dreams every night that he is a king, is as happy as a king who dreams every night he is a beggar: − but though I underscored the passage, the idea amusing me, I am not at all clear that I agree with him. Since I am on the chapter of confessions, I may as well make a whole avowal, and plead guilty to the folly of having been to consult Mme Rosa the famous necromancer, the 14th of last October. She predicted our return to Broke, told me of the disturbances we had at Leigh, and prepared my mind for the Cardinal's idiotic devotion. So far so good, I only wish I saw the rest of her prophecies drawing near their fulfilment. ——— came up perpetually in the cards, "Roquet"

[1] . . . captured by my wit and my pretty face.
[2] that boy would go far.

and "Mouvement perpetuelle"[1] as that impudent woman called him. Some intriguing mother is chasing him for her daughter, but I am happy to say, without the smallest success, as the good little fellow is very faithful to my memory, and the imaginary virtues he has thought fit to endow it with. Rosa described him with an accuracy his best friend could have found no flaw in. Kind-hearted, immensely original, exceedingly intelligent, and able to do almost anything he turns his hand to: but seeing I am perfectly aware of all these amiable attributes, I don't quite know why I'm wasting my time in writing them down. She also informed me he had been in the Engineers, which on enquiry I find to be perfectly correct: I only hope her last statement turns out wrong: two or three years will see me a widow: that point she particularly insisted on. Hélas! I am such a disbeliever in happiness in this world, that the last clause I should put great faith in, while doubting all the others.

Feb 17th

Got the most diverting letter from Aggie, detailing her last flirtation which the whole family hope will become something more, and aid and abet her accordingly. All this too for a young snob whose mother was a cook, and whose father's only a country gentleman with £5,000 a year. It makes me perfectly sick when I think of how they treated me with an earldom and £50,000 a year at stake. Enfin, there are some people of such singular obtuseness that even when past 70, they can't understand their own interests. All one can do is pity and avoid them, nothing in this wide world being as dangerous as a fool.

To come back to the subject in hand, here is my answer to Aggie and the advice she requested: — "Dearest Aggie, thanks very much for your letter, darling, which gave me the greatest pleasure. You have my entire sanction and good wishes, in your crusade against young Gore Langton's peace of mind: we have discussed matrimony too often together over the fire and manipulation of our back hair at night, for you not to be acquainted with my ideas on the subject. Some love must of course enter into the compact, but like the scriptural leaven, a very little leaveneth the whole lump — as for you individually, dear, I think it unquestionably your bounden duty, to marry

[1]*"Roquet"* means puppy, and "perpetual motion" hardly suits Morland Hutton. Is Alice thinking again of the lamented gymnast, Lord Petersham?

An evening at the Tuileries in 1867, in honour of the Czar of Russia and the King of Prussia who were visiting the Great Exhibition in Paris. Alice may well have been there. The watercolour is by Henri Baron.

Variations on the theme of Alice: pages from her album.
The colours and the dead canary suggest that the page at bottom
right may record her grief at the death of Archie.

This must have been
one of the wedding photographs
taken when Alice,
at the age of nineteen,
married George Duppa in 1870.

George Duppa.
Its position in the album
suggests that this photograph, too,
was taken at the time of
their marriage.
Though Alice chose autumnal flowers
for him, he does not look
an unattractive bridegroom.

Lady Miles and her son Cecil, whose birth coincided with that of her grandson Archie. She had already had five children (two of whom died young), but clearly made light of maternity, as she did of the passing of time.

£5,000 a year, if a merciful Providence vouchsafes you the opportunity: so 'go ahead' as the Yankees say, and in case of victory, let pink be the dominant colour in your bridesmaids' dresses, as it's particularly becoming to me. I wonder if in the course of her long scriptural researches Aunt Maria ever chanced to come across that particular parable, describing an officious individual, anxious to relieve his brother of a troublesome mote, without even remarking he was afflicted with the same infirmity? She might reflect on her own marriage, before putting you through a catechism concerning your affections – mais voilà! I dare say the idea never even occurred to her!

My last ball was at the Ellisons, some wealthy Jews, of which evening's entertainment I need only say that noses was its most prominent feature. I never congratulated myself so much on being a christian than when remarking this distinctive sign, which seems to be the birth right of every descendant of Abraham. So plain they all were too! Alas! for Torach! the daughters of Sion may sit down and weep over the departed glories, and degeneration of a race, that once gave to the world such wonders as Bathsheba, Herodias, and Mary Magdalene. I am very quiet just at present, recruiting my forces for the London season, when I mean to be quite a beauté to the furtherance of which desirable end, I sacrifice my present, and swallow an incalculable amount of nasty iron and porridge: both warranted to be strengthening and conducive to fat, a little of which would greatly improve me. The Dr has strictly forbidden anything in the shape of balls or soirées, of which there are plenty, notwithstanding Lent, and I bow very meekly to his superior wisdom, it really being too much trouble to rebel. Ah, indolence, indolence! How grateful should poor humanity be to thee, and the calming influence thou exercisest so indiscriminately; instead of which, alas, for mortal gratitude! there are some ill-advised, detestably active persons, who actually class thee in the category of vices, and exclaim at thee accordingly! All I can say is, that if indolence really be a vice, it is one that keeps half the virtues in equilibrium. I shall be very sorry not to see you in London, dear, but can scarcely say I pity you, as you seem to enjoy the pleasures of the chase, almost more in the environs of Leigh than in the heart of the great metropolis. Far be it from me to deny the charms of la chasse au général, but pleasant as it is, it cannot offer anything like the excitement of la chasse en particulière which awaits you Somersetshire way, to judge at least from your own report. Write again soon and keep me au courant of the young man's progress, as everything concerning you interests me. Best love, dear, and kisses to you — Your most affectionate cousin, Alice."

* * * * *

The Miss Boyds have been several times to see me, and I have taken a great fancy to them, they live in London and are only here en passant. Lucky mortals. Wrote to Jeanne and gave her a good lecture for saying hers was the last letter I should receive. "If that is the way you intend to give in to the obstacles you meet with in this world, I think you will have a very rough time of it, and never enjoy the success we used to speculate on together. Such a tiny obstacle as the present one is too! Mother doesn't open my letters, but insists on a post-mortem examination, so the only thing required of your laziness is to furnish me with two pieces of paper, one to be produced au besoin, the other to be suppressed! ce n'est pas plus difficile que ça! I am sorry to say the Lansdowne information is not worth the paper it's written on, only an antiquated echo of the report we are both acquainted with. That boy, my dear, is far too much in love with his own pretty face, couronne de marquis, and magnificent rent-roll to have any room left in his heart, for any less absorbing affection — and as for throwing down all these advantages at the feet of one whose conquest would not enhance his interest in any way: he would just as soon take a header into the Serpentine in his most irreproachable get-up, and daintiest grey gloves, to rescue a lady's parasol. Now Epaminondas[1] on the contrary would be capable of either of these chivalrously idiotic actions — différence de temperament!

It is a long time since I have been anywhere; my last large ball was at the Hotel de Ville, where soldiers and camellia trees were the presiding elements. 'Oh que j'aime les militaires, les militaires!' sings Mlle Schneider in the Grande Duchesse — but doubtless (to judge at least by her subsequent conduct) she had the 'Blues' generally and Lord Carrington individually in view, when relieving her mind of that sentiment. No amount of destitution in the shape of flirting materials, could I should think drive the most humble-minded of her sex to recruit her troops among the representatives of the french army, as

[1]Epaminondas, born 62 BC, a "noble character," who was a commander of the Thebans against Sparta. Hutton or Petersham? Petersham seems the more likely, since the comparison is with the rich and noble Lansdowne against whom Hutton "balances" less well.

exhibited at the Hotel de Ville that night. Some 1,000 échantillons[1] there were too, a fair number to judge from. Oh Jeanne! Jeanne! daily and hourly I bewail the unhappy fate that has pitched my tent on these hospitable, lively, albeit most uninteresting shores! Each ball I leave with a profound conviction and appreciation of my own merits, and the masculine inhabitants of Paris' utter insignificance. I fully expect I shall have become perfectly unbearable, long before I see someone sufficiently superior to myself, to lower me to my proper level. Anyhow I am candid enough to own to my enormities and moralists tell us that conviction is the first step towards amendment. Pour moi, je ne demande pas mieux que guérir![2] if wishing were all that's required I should not be surrounded by these piteous semblances of humanity long.

Did I tell you that Beckett has covered himself with glory? bolted from the Grand Hotel leaving a bill amounting to £400 and is now living in obscure lodgings with some woman, whose morals will not bear more examination than his own. You see I didn't shunt him a moment too soon. Whilst we are on the chapter of human frailty, let me tell you there are all the situations for a drama in what you wrote me of Lord Cole and Fanny Moncrieffe. She, poor girl, was, or at any rate got the credit for being very much in love with him, but when the hour of trial came, you see the beaux yeux and silvery voice of Miss Baird's money chests, proved too much for his Lordship's virtue to withstand; and after all I don't know that he is very much to be blamed, for the Enniskillen escutcheon is in pitiable want of regilding, and he may as well do it as anyone else. The Mammon of Unrighteousness is, and as far as I can make out, has always been, undisputed sovereign of this world, and we cannot be surprised when he assumes his rights and engulfs another victim. The young lady's conduct I particularly applaud, marrying the other out of pique est un beau trait[3], and sufficiently politic Arbuthnott being very well off – Mammon again! 'Put not your trust in Princes' there is the moral of the whole, and could the greatest psalmist descend for six months amongst us, he would retire to his celestial abode in disgust, at the expiration of that period, convinced that the artistocracy of our time is

---

[1]échantillons – specimens.
[2]Pour moi, je ne demande. . . .: As for me, I'd like nothing better than to improve.
[3]est un beau trait – is an inspired stroke.

not worth more than that of his own; this too after a lapse of some thousand years — and we talk about civilisation!!!

The Parisian public has had its taste for scandal tolerably well ministered to lately. First by Mlle du Hamal [?] an enterprising Hawaiian beauty, eloping with the young duc d'Aquila, the ex-king of Naples' nephew and heir, and the ignominious return of the adventurous couple, under the escort of the young man's active and irate Papa: before this fruitful subject had been half exhausted, the whole beau monde was thrown into ecstasies by a still more marvellous occurrence, nothing more or less than Mme Welles de Valette, one of the reigning beauties, M Rouher the Ministre de l'Intérieur's daughter, running away with Capoul, the prettiest tenor extant. Charming as the lady is in public, it must be concluded that her agaceries are not equally delightful tête-à-tête; certain it is that a week of the siren's society proved sufficient for Capoul, and he wrote privately to the lady's father, suggesting he should come and take the fair truant home, which was accordingly done, only this little escapade cost poor Rouher dear, as he had to pay the successful lover £2,000 for his mistress's letters, and the husband £20,000 to take her back and say nothing about it. Did you ever hear anything so disgraceful? Well may the poet exclaim:

> Argent! argent! sans toi tout est stérile
> La vertu sans argent n'est qu'un meuble inutile.[1]

That little episode I consider sufficiently startling to conclude with, all you've got to do is put your letter in the envelope I enclose, when it is safe to reach me. Adieu ma chérie, à toi toujours, Alice."

* * * * *

Now for the most extraordinary intelligence: Edith Wood, of Kelham eccentricities, is engaged to an old Essex bumpkin between 45 and 50, owner of a fine unencumbered property and £12,000 a year! and a very nice old age the poor deluded creature is, I should think, laying up for himself. Oh, Edith, Edith! va je l'admire de tout mon coeur! Talk about virtue after this, and its receiving any reward save the contemplation of its own excellence. Alas! for our degenerate age, there is no denying it, virtuous women are at a sad discount and as far

[1]Money! money! without you everything is fruitless
Virtue without money is a useless commodity.

as I can make out, likely to remain so. Tartuffe, I am delighted to hear, is ill in bed, with diphtheria — my remark is more in accordance with the rules of truth than charity — but there! it is impossible to practise every virtue!

Tuesday 9th March

The Manners Suttons are in Paris, twice I met them in the Champs Elysées, where May rode her moral hobby horse, and talked about virtue and domestic bliss, to my intense edification, more particularly as she interspersed every high-flown remark with enquiries and comments on Johnny Ogle, who I owned to having seen. It appears she has fallen into the hands of the Philistines, represented by the Woods, and the Duncan Baillies, who with that old arch-fiend de Guaris [?] for their informant, gave her an account of our way of speaking of her, and general conduct, which accounts for her present coldness. Manners, however, whose faith in my beaux yeux so long as they remain beaux, will not be easily shaken, came and paid me a long tête-à-tête visit today, during which I enlightened him as to Fanny de Guaris' two children in the country, and general line of industry, which reports he promised to spread. Unless a woman's conduct be very immaculate indeed, I shouldn't advise her to make me her enemy, as I am a singular proficient in the game of give and take, and seldom let go a chance for reprisals. My dear Retriever is well, Manners told me, and avoids the fair sex as consistently as ever. Edie Wood's marriage is broken off, because he drinks, she declares, and bearing in mind a speech where she unblushingly asserted that she'd marry the Devil himself if he'd £10,000 a year, I give her credit for too much sense to take to heart his trifling faults, and suspect the intervention of anonymous letters.

Jeudi 11 Mars

A charming concert-cotillon at the Koenigswarters. Nilsson[1] sang, and when she didn't, talked to mother and me, then there was a hideous tenor with a voice like a nightingale, and a supper where the truffles were perfection, and the champagne iced à point. I don't think

[1]Christine Nilsson, the Swedish soprano.

I ever had a greater success: "ravissante, tête de camée"[1] as one old man said. Every one of his sex at my table got introduced, and we had the merriest petit souper. What in no wise destroyed my appetite was the recollection of all the pretty little spiked malices I had occasion to inflict on Tartuffe during the evening, wreathed of course in my most plausible of smiles — Oh les femmes! les femmes! He tells me my most humble slave here is a Baron de Trelany[?]. I must look out for him!

Sat 20th March

We have had very bad news of Granny lately, and tonight my poor Dear Boy got a telegraph summoning him at once: it's just doubtful if he finds her alive.

Wed 24th March

It's all over: she died very peacefully yesterday. Poor old thing, may the Lord receive her soul! ——[2] is of course improving the shining hours of my poor Dear Boy's absence and cultivating that brute of a Tartuffe in every way. He is never out of the house. Pour moi, the moment he walks into it, I walk off to my own room, having no idea of conniving at anything so revolting. Oh dear! Oh dear! how thankful I shall be when I get away from it all. I don't know with what dominant feeling most girls begin their married life, but am perfectly convinced that mine will be gratitude, for emancipation from present evil!

Monday March 29th

Tommy Bowles came and paid us a long visit, I was quite glad to see the little monkey, he brought such a refreshing remembrance of bygones, that seem sweeter than ever when contrasted with gloomy today. I wrote the most consolatory letter to Grandpapa, full of sweet allusions to the dear departed one; it only cost me half-an-hour's thought and a large expenditure of false sentiment, whilst it is certain to please him, with whom it is my evident interest to be au mieux.

[1]ravissante, tête de camée — ravishing, like a head on a cameo.
[2]Alice's mother.

Fancy Mrs Johnny Vivian having crowned her exploits by carrying that fool of a Waterford[1] off to Barcelona in triumph, after the abortive poisoning attempt here. The husband has returned to England to try and get a divorce, which he is very unlikely to succeed in. I'm sure I trust he won't, for Waterford is quite sufficiently imbecile to marry her, which has been her aim all through: I think that scene in the Hotel must have been rich, the lover begging of the injured husband to take her back, she rushing off to take chloroform, Waterford breaking open the door only to plunge head first into an armoire à glace,[2] to the utter detriment of the dresses he had probably paid for: — Johnny Vivian's refusal to fight on the grounds that she wasn't worth it! altogether anything so fertile in comic incidents I never came across. Eloping seems to be the fashion of the day, for Tommy informs me Jimmy Lee ran away last week, with the hideous rich Miss Brady, only to be ignominiously captured and brought back to Dover. How sincerely his creditors must have regretted the unhappy occurrence!

Tuesday March 30th

Such good news I can scarcely believe it! my Dear Boy writes to say he does not like to live so far from his father and has quite made up his mind on taking a house in London; which resolution I look upon as a visible manifestation of Providence in my favour: the children though will have to be educated at home, which is an awful bore: why they can't be left at their school in Versailles I can't imagine: no such coddling fell to my lot at their age, and I don't seem to be much the worse for it.[3] Got a letter from Sydney, thanking me for the pho I gave his father, and which he of course confiscated, exactly as I intended. How delighted the poor boy will be, when he hears we're to come and live in London. Had the ineffable satisfaction of refusing to shake hands with Tartuffe, and otherwise severely snubbed him, to Mother's extreme disapproval. I could almost go wild with delight when I think that we shall soon be utterly beyond his baleful presence.

[1]Lord Waterford.
[2]A wardrobe
[3]This suggests that Alice, too, went to school at Versailles.

Wed March 31st

A most pleasant day, Mr Cay [?] such a dear little Englishman told me all about Holler [?] how the Duchess of Newcastle sent her bouquet and diamond cross to him publicly, and was hissed by the whole opera house, how he wears a bracelet with the extremely suggestive "Marguerite fleur de ma vie" etc. Tommy Bowles too was most amusing, and brought me all that has appeared of his paper [*Vanity Fair*]. I'll certainly get it bound. Dined with Ada and Julia Baddeley as normal: I have every night almost since Father's been away, not appreciating the company forced on me. Such dear girls they both are.

> *Vanity Fair* described itself as "A weekly Show of Political, Social and Literary wares". In addition to serious and satirical comment, the paper had its lighter side: one long-running spoof correspondence was between Clara Chirpaway, just plunging into high society, and her not less frivolous godmother, Tabitha Tattlefast. It's all there, balls, river picnics, inane conversations, compliments: in fact, one could almost think Alice provided the model for Clara! who, at Maidenhead, persuaded Captain Lollington to gather water-lilies for her: compare Alice's similar efforts, page 23. Also, Clara raising the question of whether Eaton Place were fashionable enough, is assured by Tabitha, "Eaton Place . . . appears . . . long, solemn, regular and dull . . . but there are all kinds of sport . . . it is not out of the way, not out of fashion." Alice, of course, first assaulted London from Lumley's base at Eaton Place. Clara writes to her touring godmother: "Italy is lovely, but Eaton Place is better!"

Thursday 1st April

Sent this letter off to Jeanne in the greatest haste: "For heaven's sake dear, put the envelope I sent you in the fire, for Laura has been larking with young men and is to be dismissed, and prepare a letter for my Dear Boy to bring me. Send full and particular accounts of Lady Mordaunt's awful row, by the side of which the Waterford affaire sinks into comparative respectability and decorum. Wales, Sir Fred Johnstone, Downe, Cole, Newport and Co, all to be had up in the Divorce Court: can't I imagine their faces and Lady Louisa Moncrieffe's!!! Yours in the greatest haste."

Mother's just heard that poor dear Mrs T—— [?] is dead — I really am sincerely sorry. The Marquis, or Marquess, as he spells it, of Lansdowne called but Mère was out. Considering the day and all, I wondered if he intended an April fool, in making the visit. If so, raise not thy hopes too high, my Lord, lest haply they be cast down. We're wiser, my book, far, than this time last year; are we not, you and I? Blanche and her sister Mrs Yorke came to see me too, and were most diverting. Such a fast little dot, the latter, given to private escapades, Pall Mall suppers, when the confiding husband thinks she's at her mother's, and improprieties of every other description. Wretched Tartuffe dined, and I managed, by dint of great exertions, to be almost more disagreeable than ever.

> "Lady Mordaunt's awful row": Sir Charles Mordaunt, MP for South Warwickshire, in 1866, married Harriet Moncrieffe, a beautiful daughter of Sir Thomas Moncrieffe. Harriet gave birth to a premature son, who was likely to become blind. Perhaps this sad event added to an existing post-natal depression, but in any event, Harriet told her husband he was not the father, but Lord Cole was, and the child's condition was due to her sins. Furthermore, she claimed she had had relationships with other men, including the Prince of Wales. The Prince was sub-poenaed to appear in Mordaunt's divorce petition, but cleared himself of suspicion. The jury decided Harriet was insane, and her confessions the result of delusions. It seems she never recovered.

Sat 3 April

Dear Boy arrived from Leigh, so exit Tartuffe, for which heaven be praised!

Friday 9th April

Went to the Bois with Mme de Plancy in her victoria and had the most interesting of conversations. She will be about my only regret on leaving this place.

Sunday 11th April

Had the greatest sport with Col. Martyn and Mrs Baddeley, both of whom are strong mediums, making tables turn after dinner. When requested to point out which of us three girls[1] would be married within the year, it bounded to me with the most singular agility. Then when questioned if my future husband were handsome, maintained a dignified silence. Is he rich, was our next enquiry, which met with an unqualified yes. Very rich? another thundering yes. Enormously rich, Col Martyn continued, and in the excitement of its feelings the table reared up on end, strewing the ground with a heap of little jetons that had been concealed in a drawer, and might easily pass for sovereigns. Whether he were noble we did not arrive at. Curious wasn't it? The only thing that surprises me, is the singular manner in which all these spirits, astronomers and sorcerers contradict each other! It informed Ada she would retain her single blessedness till 1870, but Julia would marry old Dashwood before the year's out. Enfin qui vivra verra!

Wed 21st April

Col. Martyn says he hears from London that May Manners Sutton has bolted with Johnny Ogle from Nice: idiot as she is, I can scarcely believe she'd push the science of stupidity as far as that. Besides why should she run away? They appear, to judge at least from her own avowals, and the Kelham esclandre to have gone every length without it!

Tuesday 4th May

Have been rather gay lately, as the Colonel [Martyn] is well again, and has been taking us about. Saw "Séraphine" and "Patrie", Mr Cay and Mrs Lingham accompanying us to the last. Nina, that is the lady's name, is very pretty and devoted to me. So, she tells me, is Captain Lousada [?]: also, he informed her, I was as good and pure as I am beautiful, and if he only had £20,000 a year, his one dream would be to lay it at my feet; also, that to see the manner in which I snubbed an objectionable frenchman of the name of Fieron was simply delicious, it was done with such lady-like nonchalance, and yet so completely, my looking the while just like a little queen. I must say this testimony to my undoubted abilities in that line rather pleases. Ah, Tartuffe! I will give you more than that for society and Lousada to comment on yet, never fear!

[1]Alice and Ada and Julia Baddeley.

Thursday 27th May

Nina Lingham, since I see she was the subject of my last entry, turns out to be a regular imposter: a cc[1] of the most audacious kind. I have heard nothing lately but about a certain Mr Francis Curry, the Mme de Vinchiatrou's[2] nephew, whose opinion of me is "not at all the girl to suit me!" he told his aunt, "wouldn't look at anything under a Duke, snubbed even Lansdowne last year as not good enough." I met this much-deceived young man at a dinner chez la Marquise tonight: and thought that though not the Adonis his aunt describes, considered him sufficiently goodlooking to set to work to destroy the bad impression so unconciously produced. The moss-roses in my hair were kind enough not to wither, my toilette was perfection: is it necessary to say I succeeded?

Friday 28 May

Were to have taken a note from Vinchy to her nephew but she forgot to send it to us, went up to write a message ourselves as we were in the neighbourhood, and the young man caught us on the stairs. He took us up to look at his apartment, which is simply perfect. Bedroom tendu de soie bleue. Then under his escort amused ourselves trying on diamonds in the Palais Royal[3] till 6 pm.

Sat 29th May

Met him at the Marquise's. He walked home with me and came up and admired Joy.[4]

Sun 30th May

Amused myself immensely at the races. Beauty Fane etc.

---

[1]Cocotte, presumably.
[2]Alice had some difficulty with this name, which makes it difficult to decipher; later she calls her "Vinchy".
[3]The Palais Royal at this time was full of small expensive shops.
[4]Joy: a dog perhaps? Alice later had dogs called "Fib" and "Truth".

Sat 6th June

Delicious! This week has been like a page out of London, owing to the prize at the pigeon shooting and Grand Prix, the beautiful Englishmen swarming, and beside them the french sprats dwindle down to something below even their usual inferiority. Have been nearly every day to the races and pigeons, flirted a little with Beauty Fane (who's got as far as a declaration!) and a good deal with Charlie Hambro, who dined with us the other night and sent me a lovely bouquet of gardenias. Mother has taken Wednesday evenings instead of mornings and we had a most cheerful time of it, about 40 people (Francis Curry individually) tell it not at Leigh! I've taken possession of an armchair within the inner sanctuary at the pigeon shooting, and amuse myself to the best of my abilities (no mean ones that way) with Lord Dupplin, the prettiest little viscount I've seen for a long time: it is very pleasant under these circumstances, dull as it would otherwise be! Won 5 louis under Charlie Hambro's guidance too, which were acceptable.

Friday dined with Willie Craven, Hambro, Prince de Chimay and Charles de Ligne being the other invités. Spent the morning chaperone-hunting and the afternoon talking to Vinchy's unimpressionable nephew, and Lord Dupplin over a cup of tea. Such a darling the latter is, and plays most divinely. Unhappily he leaves tomorrow night, which is another way of saying he vanishes out of my sight for ever, seeing that the jealous and astute Agatha has been playing on Father's weakness, with a running fire of abusive and threatening letters, till she has succeeded in frightening him into remaining here three years longer. Fancy giving up the city like that at the 1st call to surrender; his cowardice disgusts me fully as much as the prospect of remaining. Oh if only I was a man! In his place what a different reception such interference should meet with! Mais voilà, being a woman, all I can do is to pretend resignation, and trust to time for giving me the chance to pay them all out! Individually I may make up my mind to dress St Catherine's hair[1] for ever and ever, or marry ——, which is worse. Mon Dieu! Mon Dieu! il faut avouer ces chances là n'arrivent qu'à moi! The Grand Prix was an utter failure, dust, heat, the chance of a sun-stroke, and that was not all, for these combinations of evils and his atrocious dressing together had the

---

[1]This expression, oddly enough, means to remain celibate.

114

effect of disgusting me with ——— , my very last planche de salut.[1] Oh dear! What shall I do?

Monday 8th June

Vinchy took me with her to see the Queen of Spain. We were conducted into a petit salon and left with a whole heap of other women to wait Her Majesty's good pleasure, which would have been long and tedious in the extreme had not my guardian angel inspired the King with the idea of passing that way and fired his impressionable heart with a violent admiration for my pretty face that culminated in an order to one of his gentlemen in waiting that was transmitted to us thus: "Her Majesty the Queen is not yet disengaged, but his Majesty the King will be most happy to receive the Marquise de Vinchiaturoux and her niece, if they will pass this way." Which they accordingly did, to the surprise of all beholders, and during our three-quarters of an hour tête-à-tête the little king was most gracious. I exerted myself to the utmost for his amusement and apparently succeeded, for he did nothing but laugh, and told the Queen when she came in that he had never met anyone so spirituelle and diverting. The Queen paid me almost as many compliments and wound up by telling Vinchy her reception day was Monday, when she might come and see her, and mind and bring la ravissante petite also. So altogether our visit was very successful.

Friday 12 June

There has been a regular revolution in Paris during the last week, the military firing on the mob and lots of people killed. After Musard tonight, D———, Valentine, Belbury, George de Plancy and I adjourned to see if we couldn't see some of the fun, which we didn't succeed in, but had a charming petit souper; champagne, chicken, sandwiches, liqueur, cigarettes, till 2 am Sunday morning. It was very amusing, though perhaps not strictly correct, but then these two elements are more to be found at variance, than in harmony. D——— and I went and had tea too, in the Palais Royal during the day which I suspect Agatha would scarcely have approved of either.

[1]Planche de salut = plank clutched by a drowning man = last hope. Who this "plank" was I do not know. Beauty Fane?

29 Fbg de la Barre, Dieppe

Here we are established again in our old domicile and as far as I can see in point of society, Dieppe may hold a candle to Paris. Up to the present I have only seen a few of the natives, one Englishwoman clad in brown holland, with the traditional blue veil and waterproof, an attendant dog, several dirty children, and some uninteresting specimens of the feline race. However the time of my deliverance is at hand. Monday we start for London, and Dieppe will have plenty of time to fill up before our return which shall be as distant as I can possibly make it. Took a most delightful country drive Wednesday, and notwithstanding all my good resolutions, caught myself composing a delicious little roman on the frail foundation of that tiny note, locked so carefully away in my dressing-case. Even the marguerite I consulted whispered 'il t'aime beaucoup!'

> *Vanity Fair* gives us a lively picture of Dieppe once it had "filled up": "One of the most eligible places for idle people", with "deeper flirtations, spicier scandals" than elsewhere. At the Château d'Arques "you may lose yourself in the wood with the fairest lady of the party, and never be asked a single question when you get home". "A place," in short, "where life and morals are understood and practised as they should be."

Thursday [1st July?]

I have several times had occasion to mention that in my humble opinion there is one thing no phenomena of nature or art can ever hope to approach, and that unique object is a handsome thorough-bred Englishman. I had a pretty favourable specimen of the class introduced to me today at the Casino, Mr James Murray[1] who has only his six foot two of sufficiently solid humanity, brown eyes, and tawny moustache and beard to set against the immense disadvantage Nature inflicted when she brought him into the world as the second son of a penniless Scotch baronet. However, vu ma resignation of coiffing St Catherine, that is no sort of affair of mine, and I daresay with a little skilful management he'll do very well to help me get through the many tedious hours sure to intervene before I find anyone

[1]This "thorough-bred Englishman" was a Scot!

better. He presented me with a most lovely bouquet of roses as we left the casino, which I look upon as a pretty favourable commencement.

Saturday 3rd July

Mr Murray introduced the London ladies du grand et du demi-monde's particular pet Charlie Buller of the 2nd Life Guards. Il est joli à faire rêver[1], and singularly pleasant, the beau idéal of the detrimental Mammas so carefuly avoid; my Mother, I am happy to say, has too much sense and confidence in her daughter to do anything of the sort, and left us quite undisturbed (Sunday) to make acquaintance over his magnificent St Bernard's merits as much as we thought fit. Walked about a little too much with Mr Murray Sunday night, sufficient to entail a maternal reproof, which duly affected me. He's such a queer fellow, I can't help thinking him just a little mad, all the Murrays are! Still he pleases, and to a certain extent interests me as a new study, a curious specimen of a class I have never yet lighted on.

Monday morning, met him at the Casino at 10, and brought him home to look at the garden. It appears he is a very clever painter, and wants to do my portrait in oils, to which I have no sort of objection. Decidedly I've rather a weakness for artists. Spent the evening at the McG——'s and Mr Murray did the sweetest pencil sketch of me, to console himself with during our absence.

Tuesday 6th July

Was saluted at my arrival in London tonight with the pleasing intelligence of —— 's marriage. How very grateful Miss La [?] Carrington should be to my grandmother! That's all the remarks I have to make on the subject. Despatched M—— a letter with the significative PS "I quite expect your answer to be in person." Posted it Wed morning, so I ought either to hear from or see him Friday at the earliest. Spent such a stupid day, Wed and Thursday, going to see "The Turn of the Tide" the dullest piece ever written or represented during the dog days. Fought just a little with Minnie Vaughn too — the heat and idleness make one pugnacious!

---

[1] Il est joli. . . : He's a dream of beauty.

Lord Petersham married Eva, daughter of Lord Carrington. It was Alice's style to make a show of not caring when she met with a disappointment (indeed her diary will soon show that it did not take her long to persuade herself, as well as others, that she was above being hurt). In this case, however, she was probably genuinely more concerned with the prospect of seeing Moreland Hutton again than she was with the news of Petersham's marriage. However likeable he was, he had clearly represented "every girl's duty" rather than a strong attraction, and anyway she knew that she had already lost her chance with him.

Friday 9th July

What idiot ever discovered that Fridays were unlucky? It's a perfect mistake, for as far as I am concerned I have not been so happy this year as today. Came back after rather a dull turn in the Park just in time to catch Lionel[1]. When he'd gone I settled myself cozily on the sofa with a book, but somehow the remembrance that it was Friday and the bare possibility of M—— appearing would persist in obtruding itself between me and the pages. I gave up my attempt to read at last in despair, and resigned myself to my thoughts, till a ring at the bell, followed by White's announcing "Mr ——" brought me most pleasantly from speculation to reality. Isn't it funny, when he was there, I couldn't find a word to say and we sat staring at each other like idiots, till Mother came to the rescue. (Memorandum: I must hold myself on my guard; I don't like this dumb symptom: its very novelty is dangerous.) The Col and Mother went out about 4 and we spent the remainder of the afternoon together: he is looking so handsome, and appears taller than ever, after all those french shrimps. It was so sweet of him to come too all the way from —— to see me. Dear! How I bless the instinct that prompted me to write. The person I'd not bless though, is his mother; a nice vixen she appears to be, judging from his own account, her one aim and object in life being to prevent him marrying, in which a success attends her efforts that they utterly undeserve. "My mother would sooner see me in any species of danger than sitting on this sofa with you" he told me tonight. In that case, and standing in such righteous awe of her as he evidently does, why on earth did he come all this way to see me? The sooner he goes, under

[1]Probably Lionel Massey.

such circumstances, I think the better: for shall I confess it to you my little book, I like him a great deal too much as it is. He is so good, and handsome, and earnest in all he says; so different to the vapid young scamps my life has lain amongst up to the present, and who I am so unutterably weary of. A coronet is a very pleasant thing in its way, but I wonder if it's worth a man like this? Shall I tell a fib as I do to my friends and relations and say yes? Or shall I for once put down what I really think, no! Dear me, the word has escaped me, and as it would make a smudge on this nice clean paper to scratch it out, I may as well leave it there. Notwithstanding that confession I must just dismiss him from my mind, seeing he told me pretty plainly tonight, thanks to his mother, he could not marry during his father's lifetime. By the time he is free, what will my name be, I wonder? Lady Willoughby, perhaps, who knows?

Such a lot of stupid people dined, but he came and talked to me all the evening. He! He! There I am again! bah! let me shut my book, or I shall actually catch myself en flagrant délit of talking sentiment, and sentiment is a luxury only heiresses can afford to indulge in.

Sat 10 July

He met us in the Park and with the Kers [?] we made a very pleasant little party. What a strange fellow he is to be sure. Declared he must go home this afternon, couldn't come to Hampton Court with us tomorrow, and altogether was decidedly disagreeable, till I said I'd take Lionel instead, when he suddenly retracted, and became perfectly amenable. Tommy Bowles came and talked to me a little and the two glared at each other: in the most approved style, only fancy they cut each other dead! Such, little idiot, is Tommy's spite and jealousy. Spent the most charming day at Hurlingham surrounded by all my ancient adorers, with Lord Dupplin the new favourite at their head. We went and had tea together: returned on Mr Tufton's dray. Mr —— wasn't there, as he couldn't find any member to introduce him, which absurd rule, it appears, is strictly enforced. Went to the opera in the evening. Patti was delicious in "Dinorah",[1] Lord Dupplin de service again, that is, he saw me to the carriage and generally made himself useful.

[1]An opera by Meyerbeer – described by Kobbé in his *Complete Opera Book* as less a pastoral than pasteurised.

Sunday 11th July

Spent such a delicious day at Hampton Court, is it necessary to say, with Mr —— ? Laying lazily under the trees, watching the gold fish swim in and out among the water lilies, talking or being still just as the spirit moved us. "The greatest sacrifice a woman can make to a man" I remember telling him, "is the sacrifice of her other adorers." "A woman who could not do so is worth nothing," was his somewhat sharp reply. How strange he is to be sure: today he was amiable, disagreeable, rough, caressant, all in the same breath. He put me so out of patience at last, that coming home in the train I treated him to the history of a fictitious Jew.[1] We had to walk from Vauxhall to Victoria finding no cab: and for those two hours he was as sweet as possible: stroking the hand on his arm, and owning to having kept carefully the letter I wrote to him. Even then though he must needs declare it was for its scent of roses. I wonder if he expected me to believe it! Oh, dear, I should like to know if he really is fond of me? Sometimes I almost think so − and yet − !

Monday 12 July

A great deal too hot to do anything but lay on the sofa in an artistically darkened room with Mr —— to amuse me, which innocent little diversion I was unfortunately debarred from, as the gentleman in question left London at 9 am. Business took him away as usual. Business, faugh! I hate the very word, interfering in this brutal manner with my enjoyment. Depend upon it, the drones of society are the proper persons to choose one's admirers from and if Mr —— ever fails me I'll take care his successor has nothing to do but run hither and thither at my behest, undisturbed by fluctuations in railway shares, Manchester meetings and the state of the crops.

Passed the evening at the French play, where they gave the first representation of "Orphée aux Enfers".[2] Here's The Times' opinion on Mlle Schneider's final pas: "The most outrageous can-can that ever desecrated the London stage, is towards the end of the first act, danced by the whole company, and rapturously encored," which shows – n'en deplaise a la morale! – the British public are awakening

---

[1] I can offer no explanation of this mystifying "history".

[2] *Orpheus in the Underworld* by Offenbach, premiered in Paris in 1858, came to the St James Theatre in London in 1869 with Hortense Schneider.

to a sense of their own past absurdity, and trying to overcome the inane prejudices that caused it.

Tuesday 13th July

D—— and I were so admired at the opera, never was there anything like it. During every entr'acte we were surrounded with men: I must say such universal adulation is very enjoyable! "Martyn's two beauties", is the name an appreciating public have discerned[1] to us.

Wed 14th July

The Baddeleys called, and Julia tells me a friend of hers saw me last night at the opera and raves of nothing else. "She was leaning slightly forward," he exclaimed, "her hand resting on the back of my chair, listening intently to La Patti, and watching the rapt interest on her lovely face, feeling that little white hand so near me, it was all I could do to prevent myself stooping down and touching it with my lips!" Did you ever hear anything like that! Julia will tell him I am going back next Saturday, and make him wear a white marguerite in his buttonhole that I may recognise him. Really such profound admiration deserves at least an answering look.

Monday 19 July

Went and looked at the pho I gave M—— which he has had painted, it really is very pretty. Had tea with Mrs Hobhouse, and stood a long time in the Park, with Mr Montgomery one side of the carriage and Denison the other. Lionel paid me a visit, he leaves tomorrow for Ireland — hélas!

Thurs 22nd July

"Baby" Dupplin paid me a long visit, then I went out driving with Miss Dickson and took her to look at M—— 's photo. It seems so extraordinary that he should have taken no sort of notice of the letter I wrote nearly a week ago, that knowing his mother's character, and

[1]"Discerned" — Alice is muddling her English and French. In French "décerner" is to award or bestow.

judging her to be quite capable of dexterously making away with any suspicious-looking epistle, I took the precaution of writing our Dieppe address at the back of the photo, with an enquiry in french, whether he ever received my letter, then gave it back to the shopman with the injunction to send it as soon as possible. Voilà madame! if you have been trying unfair play, you calculated without the least knowledge of your adversary's strength, and I think I have check-mated you very prettily.

Sat 24th July

Got the nastiest letter from M—— this morning, evidently written in one of his very worst moods, simply stating business kept him from coming to London, without adding one regret or pretty message, as honey to digest this very unpalatable crust. Spent all morning in composing indignant answers I put in the fire as soon as written with the reflection that a disdainful silence is more aggravating than responses, arguing as it does "That indifference which piques each chevalier as it ought, of all offences that's the worst offence, which seems to state you are not worth a thought." Besides, my indignation will keep, as he will duly experience at our next meeting. Having then wasted about a quire of dainty pink paper (which shall also not be forgotten when the hour of reckoning comes!) it occurred to me that I might possibly discover a way of spending my time more profitably, both as regards my amusement and interest. Accordingly I announced my intention of going to Hurlingham. Father went off to his club to see if any of his friends with drays were going and would take us, and returned triumphantly with Col. Dickson, a remarkably goodlooking 16th Lancer who promoted me to the seat on the box next to him, and did his very best to amuse me all day. There was scarcely anyone at Hurlingham, but as Col. Dickson never left me, I found it very pleasant indeed: need I say que dans mes mauvais dispositions vers M—— , I tried to leave him with as good an opinion as he inspired me with and I think I succeeded. Found Lord Dupplin waiting for me when I got home, but had to send him away as it was ¼ to 8, and I had barely time to dress for dinner. He descended from his box though, at the opera, and took possession of a stall next to me, till at the 2nd entr'acte that odious Pepys came and turned him out. Mother was not well enough to go and the Col in a truly diabolical humour. Lord John Hayes and the Marquis of Graham were introduced.

Sunday 25th July

The Colonel still perfectly unbearable because I would not go and spend the day at Hampton Court with him and an intensely uninteresting party of elders, for the three very excellent reasons; of my being anything but well; having disposed of my time quite differently; and being averse to destroy the remembrance of the charming day passed there so lately. Perhaps the third reason was the most decisive, anyway I braved my host's wrath, stayed at home, et bien m'en a trouvé, everything happened just as arranged. First Leila and Calcraft arrived then Creyke, who treated me to a sentimental treatise till Lord Dupplin came and turned him out. That pretty baby even announced his intention of staying and dining with me tête-à-tête, but I wouldn't have him. As it is, I was much more amiable than I should have been, without my indignation towards M—— or than he in any wise deserved. He got very pathetic saying goodbye, and promised to join me at Dieppe: a statement with all respect to his veracity be it said, I don't implicitly believe in.

Monday 26th July

Went out driving with Mrs Hobhouse, which was anything but lively.

Thursday 29th July

Returned to Dieppe and for the first time in my life I think I was thoroughly glad to leave London. Everybody was so glad to see us, it was quite delightful.

[Letter to Jeanne, August 6th 1869]

Bien Chère: we left the delights of England's smoky metropolis 8 o'clock the Thursday before last and for the first time in my life I did not moan or lament. Goodwood had cleared out everybody, except a few wretched Foreign Office attachés and disconsolate Guardsmen, who couldn't get leave. Conversation with the latter under such circumstances has been impossible, they did nothing but pace up and down the room reviling their hard fate, stare out of the window and wonder "why the deuce a fellah should be put upon in such a way" and restlessly hope Jim, Frank or Charlie hadn't forgotten to back

"Brigantine" for them; and take any odds they could get against the field. You ask for the latest news: Lady Mordaunt's case is adjourned to November which I look upon as a master-stroke of Lady Louise's, as we shall be well into the shooting season then, and even scandal recedes baffled into the background, when weighed in the scales of the masculine mind with partridges, grouse, pheasants and woodcock. Lord Cole in mortal terror of perhaps in the event of a divorce taking place, being dragged into becoming the fair delinquent's happy number 2, hardened his heart to the extent necessary to lead the ugliest Miss Baird to the altar. Having raised her to the rank of Viscountess though, there I suppose he considered his obligations ended, since three days after his marriage he was seen wandering disconsolately in the Park with the expression of a man who has arrived at l'été de St Martin's dreariest days, instead of being still in the first rosy flush of la lune de miel. As for Waterford and Vivian, that has quite faded into a thing of the past, and scarcely provokes now a blush from some over-hypocritical ingénue, or warning "hush! hush! my dear, don't you see the girls!" from the Dowager in command. Then we had the marriage of the Marquis of Huntly to Miss Cunliffe Brooke, who [Huntly] philosophically reflecting "noblesse" was "obliged" so long, it surely need oblige no longer, seized the first opportunity of introducing a little good plebian blood and plebian gold, into the noble but impoverished family. Mr Brooke when asked what he thought of his son-in-law replied "I do like 'Untly, he is so very h'aristocratic," and as the "h'aristocratic 'Untly" the poor young man has been known ever since. To quit the regions of scandal and return to my own affairs up to the present I find Dieppe very bearable (suppressed as not prudent:)[1]. Ever since I heard that story Sicilly H—— [2] was the undignified hero of, such is the fond de canaillerie[3] really existing if you only dig deep enough for it, in every female mind, I have been secretly wishing to meet someone like him, et enfin j'ai trouve! Cis en beau,[3] though; Cis surrounded with all the prestige an immense fortune recklessly squandered, Don Juan's reputation, and several duels éclatants[3] bestows. Instigated, if I am to believe him, by

---

[1] "Suppressed as not prudent" – words added by Alice, but is it not clear how much of what follows was omitted from her letter to Jeanne.
[2] Sir Cecil Heneage – "Sicilly" presumably a nickname. Upper-class accents tended to turn Cecil into Cicil.
[3] "fond de canaillerie" – bottom of vulgarity; "Cis en beau" – an improved version of Cis; "duels éclatants" – notorious duels.

an overwhelming passion 2 years concealed, though I should rather say by the exciting influence of the sea-breezes and Dieppe dullness, this dangerous young man took to making love to me, and faute de mieux de faire, really caught the malady he intended inoculating me with. For 4 days matters did not progress very smoothly, but still they progressed: at the end of that time he got so terribly in earnest, that actuated by the most prudential motives and with Cis's wholesome example before my eyes, I found myself constrained to give him his congé. Instead of receiving it in a humble and contrite spirit, this very misguided young man now thinks fit to placard an outrageous misery, the more absurd that none of his sex have the physical capability of experiencing it; only he is wonderfully eloquent, not particular in sticking to truth, where a detail added or effaced would embellish history, and killingly handsome, Mother has chosen to espouse his cause, and morning, noon and night, I am harangued about my "infamous conduct" till I almost wish it had been infamous, when at least I should have reaped a certain amount of amusement. Altogether the whole episode, notwithstanding my prudence, would do very well to turn into a short but thrilling romance headed "Une passion aux eaux." Suppose I undertake it and have it ready for inspection at the next meeting? I just see Vivian got his divorce, and the next thing we shall hear, I suppose, is of Madame receding from the horizon with a couronne de marquis to grace her retreating brows! From a strictly philosophical view I can't help wondering of what good that superfluous article known as "virtue" is, in the 19th century? Goodbye, dear; now, write to me very soon, your ever affectionate, Alice.

Alice enlivened most of August with a further entanglement with this "dangerous young man". However, having reduced him to quivering passion and rage, she extricated herself by embarking on a sailing cruise — with her mother, naturally. His name was Georges d'Trisson.

Sea Breezes and a Resolution

The Sea Bird, Dartmouth, Saturday 27th August

HE die is cast, we actually did make up our minds and sailed last Thursday from Dieppe, arriving here yesterday at 1½ pm, after about 24 hours of passage the Capt. was kind enough to call smooth, but which, had my opinion been requested, I should have described as quite the reverse, seeing we heaved and pitched about the whole time, as did never that much maligned article "steamer". I just saved my reputation by not being ill, but must plead guilty to feeling very uncomfortable, and being equal to nothing but perfect quiet on a sofa with Monceau[1] to read poetry to me, and administer an occasional

[1]The Belgian Comte de Monceau, owner of *The Sea Bird*.

B & S.[1] The two things don't sound quite congenial, do they? and indeed I never was as indifferent to the dulcet strains of Alfred de Musset and as cognisant of the merits of "Hennessy's Fine Champagne" in all my life before.

Our present quarters are quite lovely, nothing can be more picturesque than the broad blue river, with here and there a white sail dotting the surface, lying between miles radiant with cornfields, and masses of dark green foliage; nothing I suppose can be more romantic than the calm starlit nights, with only the melodious plashing of the water, and a distant echo of some sailor's song, breaking the universal stillness. Any stranger passing and marking Monceau's lover-like pose and manner, as he reclines on a cushion at my feet would, were he prosaic, murmur "lucky devils" or were he reflective, arrive at the conclusion that the one thing invariably lacking to every otherwise perfect situation in life, was surely not lacking here, and pursue his way reflecting on the last time the lines had fallen unto him in equally pleasant places: retrospection, when agréable, is not wanting in certain charms, so I will respect it only, gentle stranger, in this one instance. Your perspicacity is utterly at fault. That Monsieur le Comte is very much to be envied there is no doubt; but that the object of his affections has already begun to look wearily at a certain star sacred to someone else, got slightly tired of his devotion, and commenced to wish herself back at Dieppe again, is equally certain. With another person, who shall be nameless, in Monsieur's place I can scarcely imagine anything more delicious than this pleasurable indolent existence, but as it is! well, as it is, Félix (we all call each other by our Christian names, ceremony being a thing appertaining to land, and on the seas unknown) Félix is a decided nuisance, and an enterprising nuisance, which is the very worst style of all. I never agreed with the sage who declared that the attentions of an admirer one dislikes, are worse than his neglect, but I declare another week of M le Comte's society will convert me to his opinion. I never have a moment to myself from 8 o'clock in the morning till 12 at night. The morals of our floating residence are so strangely − what shall I call it? primitif! the fear and trembling with which we dress and undress would surprise the uninitiated: such an article as a bolt doesn't exist, locks indeed there are, but all the keys have been carefully withdrawn! A severe scratch down the face and several uncompromising

[1]B & S − brandy and soda.

bruises have at last begun to reduce F—— into something like order, the opaqueness of the masculine intelligence is really extraordinary, that such manifestations are necessary to convince them No, in a woman's mouth, doesn't always mean Yes! "Big Jim", such a handsome sailor, nearly got his marching orders, for giving it as his opinion that "the Master is awfully in love with the pretty young lady, and worrits her dreadful sometimes I'm sure, poor little dear, so much as I should be tempted to go in and give him one over the h'eye, if he began when I was there!" With all thanks to handsome "Jim" for his friendly intentions, the "pretty young lady" is admirably able to take care of herself and keep the rebellious Belgian at a safe, if not respectful distance. C'est égal, si jamais on me rattrappe sur un yacht![1]

Did I say poor Murray was most tender at the Milner Gibsons'[2] ball, the night before we started on this mad-cap expedition, made me a solemn declaration of affection, and actually wanted to propose! "You know what I am going to say next" he whispered after some most affectionate speech, "may I?" "I think you had better not," was my prudent answer, "as it would only give unnecessary pain to both." Wasn't that rather a pretty way of putting him off? He also informed me he had chosen seconds in the event of F—— persisting in his sanguinary designs, and only waited the shadow of provocation. Poor honest Jim![3] what short work the revengeful frenchman would make of him to be sure; and what fools men are to hate each other like this, because of a woman who doesn't care twopence for either of them. My heart being asleep did not prevent my intelligence being thoroughly on the alert, and I give myself great credit for having kept them apart so successfully.

I am sitting on the floor of my cabin writing this and it is quite pleasant even with pen and ink to retrace a little excitement; this evening has been so woefully dull, Félix sulking under my wholesome discipline, Jules making love to Mother, and the Dear Boy getting generally in everybody's way. Avec cela the wind is howling, and tomorrow we sail where Providence and the tides alone can tell!

---

[1]C'est égal. . . : All the same, catch me being caught on a yacht ever again!
[2]Milner Gibson was Tommy Bowles's father.
[3]James Murray, not "Big Jim" the sailor.

Sea Breezes and a Resolution

Wed 1st Sept.

After mature deliberation I have come to the conclusion that for the warning and instruction of all unwary passengers "ci fit la vertu"[1] should be printed in legible type over the bulwark of every yacht; then if they chose to affront the unknown dangers that mysterious inscription shadowed forth, by all means let them do so; and the consequences of such temerity be upon their own heads; as for poor deluded innocents like ourselves, sympathy cannot be too largely lavished on them. Mais voilà, non parlons plus, however unconsciously a person stumbles on a wasps' nest, they can scarcely hope to escape without a few stings. Yesterday was pleasant enough, going down the river, missing the boat, and coming back by carriage, it being too rough to start from Dartmouth for good and all; as for today, it was simply unbearable. Tears in the morning, scenes in the afternoon, and a stupid walk to wind up all. Je ne vous dis que ça!

Thurs 2 Sept.

Left Dartmouth in a gale of wind and on the whole stood it capitally, not even feeling uncomfortable, though of course I laid [*sic*] upon the sofa, and let Félix feed me; it pleases him so immensely and on the whole doesn't do me any material harm. Arrived at Ryde 2½ Friday afternoon, and went on shore at once, met Ada Baddeley who came on board during dinner. Félix had the gig out to take them back and insisted on me accompanying him. That I really did enjoy, it was extremely rough and each mountainous wave that came towards us, looked as if it must engulf our boat, and wash us all away. The mere possibility of danger brings with it an exquisite pleasure nothing else affords, I forgot all about my uninteresting companion, and his systematic persecution as I sat quite still watching the huge rolls of water coming, and the sparkling of the phosphorus following each dip of the sailors' oars: on the whole I think Félix was gladder to reach the Sea Bird again than I was: provoked perhaps by his words and protestations I could not join in, an intense craving for a little physical excitement had taken possession of me, and the dusting about [?] we got from Mother Ocean did me good. Oh if only Mr —— had been there, what a delicious night it would have been!

[1]"Virtue beware!"

Sat 4th Sept

Went and had a group done at Jabez Hughes: Félix, Jules, D——,
Dear Boy and I. Then gave our young men the slip to their intense
disgust and went off with the Baddeleys: Julia tells me she has got
over her grande passion for old Dashwood but only to tumble into
another for a feline-looking Russian, who by all I can make out,
appears to be a proper scamp: elle est désespérante de bêtise, cette
petite là.[1]

Had great sport on the pier watching the humble devotion of a Mr
Stirling or some such name, who was knocked over at once by my Sea
Bird hat and the face it sheltered. The empressement with which he
picked up a withered bouquet of myrtle I had in the bosom of my
dress, and threw away was good to see; altogether I spent a pleasant
day, dined with the Baddeleys and returned to the Sea Bird towards
10½. Leaned over the bulwarks a long time looking down into the
water before I went to bed; for tomorrow we return to Dieppe, and
though I shall be most glad to get rid of Félix, I am half sorry to leave
the yacht, that delicious gurgling of water round our boat, and the
gentle rocking that sends me so pleasantly to sleep, I shall particularly
miss; but enough of regrets, here comes Félix, and I must go below if I
don't want to be worried with him for the next half-hour, so goodbye
dear Sea Bird and fair Mother Ocean, I shall not forget the pleasant
time I have spent on both.

Monday 6th Sept. Dieppe.

Got back here after a most atrocious passage – which I didn't mind,
and a wearisome journey, which I did.

Mon 20th Sept

Found the Casino just a little bit dull without Fred,[2] that odious child
Clarence Collier tried giving impudence about him again, but a
wholesome application of my right hand to his left ear, stopped him
summarily. Fancy the other day his attacking him with, "I say Sir,

---

[1] She's quite appallingly silly, that child.
[2] Sir Frederick des Voeux, a "diminutive but sufficiently agreeable little
Guardsman".

aren't you awfully in love with Miss Miles? It's no good saying you're not, you know, for the whole plage is talking of it." I'm afraid the Coldstream Guards would have blushed for their comrade, had they seen the sudden crimson flush with which his whole face bore witness to the accusation. I felt very much inclined to laugh, but checked it and looked the other way, blessed being the merciful.

Mon 27th September

Alone with my own ideas and the waves, undisturbed by man or beast; I have been thinking very seriously this week and here are the results of my meditation summed-up in the most business-like of letters to Father: "Dear Boy; after mature deliberation I have come to the conclusion that I cannot go on living in Paris, unless absolutely obliged. Physically it doesn't agree with me, seeing I manage to die, nearly, every winter of bronchitis, and morally it is doing away with the few good principles that have survived 6 years of it, as rapidly as it can. Therefore I have quite made up my mind to take up my quarters at Leigh if grandpapa will have me, and giving up the 'sinful lusts of the flesh' devote myself to look after him. I have no illusions regarding the sort of life I shall lead, I know it will be a species of acted torpor, but still I have made up my mind to it, and at any rate it will be accustoming myself to what is more than probable I shall have to undergo in the future with that 'country clergyman' you are so fond of alluding to, and morally and physically it will be far more healthy than the species of false existence I am leading now, and wish so much to escape from. Mother has given her consent, so I just want you to propose it as prettily as you can to Grandpapa. I am sure he ought to be very glad to have some companion in his solitude, and if he thinks he's rescuing a soul from that 'den of iniquity Paris' he'll jump at it at once. I will send you an insinuating letter for him to back you up, but it's a thousand pities I can't see him, when the coaxing he has always given in to would settle the matter in a quarter of an hour. If you were really a very dear Boy, you would let me come over to you, anyhow try and settle it: I would go to him in the beginning of December when we leave Colonel Martyn: the advantage of having me on guard en permanence to disperse the wiles of the evil one, as represented by Agatha, Mary and Maria, I need not enlarge on. Mother goes to Paris tomorrow, I put off that evil moment as long as possible and remain till the 6th. Miss Roch has triumphantly proved the existence of the

1st Mrs Burton, so they are going to bring an action for bigamy against the wicked old Dr and the fair Jane is a spinster open to the allurements of matrimony again. Goodbye, Dear Boy, your affectionate Alice."

Sunday Oct 3rd

Got a very sweet letter from the Dear Boy, quite approving the Leigh plan and saying he would propose it to Grandpapa: so I despatched him the following most diplomatic epistle, as credentials. "Dearest Grandpapa; of course you will have heard that Father has quite determined on continuing to live in Paris, which I sincerely regret, as neither morally nor physically does it agree with me. All the Drs are unanimous in declaring that the winters are too cold for my chest, besides even putting that entirely out of the question, I am very unhappy there. Grandpapa dear, you must be lonely at Leigh all by yourself, so why shouldn't I come and stop with you? I think you would find it pleasanter with a companion, and if you will only have me, I am sure my affection for you will soon show me how to please you in all things. It would be so nice for both of us, and of such infinite advantage in a religious point of view to me. However pure it is the life one leads in town can never be what it is in the country where the tiniest blade of grass your feet crush, or one of the many sweet blossoms round you recall daily and hourly the mighty works of God, and his infinite goodness in making the world so beautiful. I feel this painfully sometimes and long – oh more than I can tell you dear Grandpapa, to get away from noisy frivolous Paris and find myself alone a little with Nature and the great lessons she teaches. If you think that I should bore you, write and tell me so; only do you know Grandpapa, you have always been so kind to me, I don't think I should; on the contrary, I am convinced that after a week or two, you would find me a very handy little housekeeper: try and see if you do not become a convert to my opinion. We leave Dieppe Tuesday so direct to Paris – there is not a living soul here, but the weather is so lovely, the sea such a beautiful blue placid lake, that I am quite sorry to leave it. Goodbye dear Grandpapa, with fondest love and kisses, I am ever your most affectionate grandchild, Alice Catherine Miles."

* * * * *

There! If that diplomatic effusion doesn't gain me that point, then it ought to. I have been so miserable thinking about M—— lately and fearing that the amiable tongues of this world should prate about my empty french life, till they turned him against me, that I have absolutely been driven to this strong measure in self defence. If I see him, I shall explain my whole reasons, and then he must believe there is some good in me, to cut the whole concern, and rusticate of my own accord in the country, just to preserve his high opinion.

Went to Vespers to St Rémy which I am very fond of doing. The solemn hush of the grand old catholic cathedral, with only the full rich tones of the organ breaking the cloistral stillness, the lighted candles gleaming on the altar that contrast so strangely with the afternoon sunbeams, that dyed in every rich hue of crimson, gold and purple, from passing through the stained glass windows, fall like an aureole on the heads of the prostrate worshippers below: all impress me strangely and give me some half hour or so of calm and solitude, inexpressibly soothing after the wear and tear of life. Such peaceful thoughts as are awakened by the very sanctity of the edifice, and lulled by the monotonous chant of the officiating priest — one cannot but believe in the efficacy of prayer amongst this kneeling throng of worshippers, however the broad glare of daylight disperse the pleasant faith. To me, these catholic churches are bright oases in the desert of life, where it is very sweet to linger, when like Pilate one almost begins to ask "what is truth?" and longs wearily for some rest to mind or body, feeling this burden almost greater than one can bear. Today I found myself sitting in a queer dark corner near the entrance, between a lot of picturesque fisher-children and their grandmother, an old hag wrinkled till scarcely a feature was discernible, with simple piety many might take a lesson from, crooning over her beads. Had I gone further I might have got into far more aristocratic quarters, but I preferred remaining where I was, and kneeling down among these humble fishers, prayed oh! so earnestly! for guidance and strength to act aright, in the difficult position where I am now placed: — one name was often whispered in my supplications and I hope bore them up to heaven. Oh could I look on only just a little and see its end!

Wed 6th October

Packed the poor children back to school and returned to Paris. Found Mother suffering from a bad throat and unable to go out.

Thurs 7th Oct

Went to see "Perlipinpin[?]" at the Chatêlet with Jane and at our return towards 12½ nearly dead with sleep and laughter found the following most awakening and sobering epistle from grandpapa. "My dear Alice — your Father has just given me your letter, which I lose not a moment in answering. Come my love, and live with me during my life, if it so pleases you, but recollect that after my loss, and at my age, you can have but little gaiety and amusement and that almost my sole society is the members of my own family. Yet if you like to come you will receive the heartiest welcome and I shall be always glad to give you such advice" etc — from your knowledge of dear old Sir William, it will not be difficult, my book, to guess the not much good advice, a tirade on the beauty of truth, followed by an account of my aunt's christian virtues, which scarcely tallied with it, another warm welcome and his signature. And now my little confidante, that we are in possession of the leading facts of the letter: let us sit down and think what we shall do. First I must confess to having cried myself to sleep over it, though why I should cry over getting my own way, is a feminine contradiction I am powerless to explain. Second I wrote and accepted his kind offer in the most grateful terms: I must try and gain sufficient influence over him to give M—— the run of Leigh, and that never could be done, without taking him in hand personally; so goodbye to flirtation, congenial companionship, conversation, all in short that makes life endurable for six long weary months, et vogue la galère of dullness and ennui[1]. A most trustworthy proverb assures us "que celui qui veut la fin, veut les moyens" —[2] when I think of the "fin" for the mere chance of which I am willing to go through all this, I am frightened at perceiving how infinitely precious to me it has become, domineering my every thought and action; how different to the ambitious longing I once entertained for a coronet and dignified by a higher finer name. My book, what shall I do if I can't see him in November, if he fails me, in short? Thinking of it now, it seems as if I could never bear it, and yet I suppose I should, as others have done before, and will do afterwards for alas! I am not romantic and don't believe in people dying of misplaced affection and broken hearts; depend upon it, on that subject Byron's view, though cynic, is the correct one —

[1]et vogue . . . ennui: and let's chance dullness and boredom.
[2]"que celui qui veut . . . .": the end justifies the means.

Taught to consent, their bursting hearts despair
Over their idols, till some wealthier lust
Buys them in marriage — and what rests beyond?
A thankless husband, next a faithless lover,
Then dressing, nursing, praying, and all's over!

Sunday 17th October

I am nineteen today and anyhow have the consolation of beginning this new year with a bit of good news. Col. Martyn has promised to ask M—— to come and shoot with him this winter and now I am trying hard to persuade Mother to write and tell him, that he may not engage himself. She says she will, but I own I shall not be quite easy until I see the letter written.

Saturday 30th October

Here are the results of an hour's meditation this morning, before I got up: "L'espérance ressemble en tous points à une maîtresse qui ne nous aime pas. Elle commence en nous faisant entrevoir des félicités divines, mais elle finit toujours par nous tromper."[1] After that brief exposition of my ideas, it is scarcely necessary to say my 19th[2] year has not begun more favourably than my 18th, 17th or sixteenth, and things persist as usual in going radically wrong, in spite of my efforts at conciliation and arrangement. When towards 10½ I did get up, a most melancholy prospect met my eyes and I might had I been poetically disposed have written with Longfellow:

> The day is dark and cold and dreary
> It rains and the rain is never weary.

ending up with a cunningly-wrought comparison between the weather and my life except that I don't quite believe in the reality of sorrows that adapt themselves to metre, and compress themselves into rhyme; and it always struck me that throughout the elaborate divinity of 15 epistles and 4 gospels, there is not one sentence that comes home to the heart of the reader like that tiny verse in which St John tells us that

---

[1]"Hope is exactly like a mistress who does not return our love. She begins by giving us glimpses of divine delights, but she always ends by deceiving us."
[2]She had just had her nineteenth birthday, so it was her twentieth year.

over the grave of Lazarus his friend "Jesus wept." To come at once to my chapter of grievances, after many détours, and at the expense of as many blushes as would set up any ordinary ingénue for a year, I at last persuaded Mother to write and tell M—— of our Colonel's intention of asking him to Broke the first week in December — here's his answer. "Dear Mrs Miles — It is very kind of you to tell me of Col Martyn's invitation and I should like the visit greatly, but unfortunately it is the week of our shooting at home, and that I cannot leave. I am at present incapacitated from either hunting or shooting from the result of two trifling accidents; how long I shall be in this melancholy condition, I don't know. I expect I shall be in London about the end of the month, when I hope to see you. With many thanks and kind remembrances to Mr and Miss Miles, believe me yours very truly etc ——".

Sufficiently unsatisfactory that, isn't it, but nothing to what is coming. From his ten days' delay in answering Mother's letter it was evident to me that he had tried to put off his own shooting and not succeeded, probably because of that bothering brother, and mentally resolving to pitch into him well in London, gradually relent, and make Col. Martyn ask him for the second week instead of the first.[1] I dismissed the subject from my mind, with my estimate either of his willingness or intelligence slightly lowered it is true, but still with no doubts of ultimately succeeding; when lo! a brutal Leigh letter comes and upsets all my plans, by making us leave Paris a week later, thus depriving us of our ten days in London, preventing me seeing M—— and utterly routing my skilfully contrived combinaisons. I can still make the Col. write to him, it is true, but what's a letter without an interview to back it up: all the documents that ever passed through the hands of her gracious Majesty's scarlet-coated officials, were never worth ten minutes tête-à-tête; and pages of written eloquence never did or will produce the same effect as the "please do" when properly accentuated. May who I took counsel with in my perplexity suggested me writing again, but that I don't like to do: I am so afraid of his thinking I am running after him, and then with the short-sightedness of his sex, imputing my empressement to his being heir to a large fortune. Hang those uncompromising thousands, say I! It's not a ladylike expression I know, but at present they are dreadfully in my

[1]Alice was writing very fast, and the grammar of this sentence has gone to pieces.

way, and though I daresay he wouldn't thank me for my charitable intentions I sincerely wish I could change him into a penniless Guardsman, or out-of-elbows foreign office attaché. Well, well! I suppose it's all fate, and now Leigh has come interfering again, I may as well abandon my poor little hopes to be swallowed up in the vast shipwreck which generally overtakes such frail embarcations. "Kismet" as the Mahomedans would say, and in the face of wind and tide, it's no sort of use wasting one's strength and energy struggling against it.

Monday 1st November

Mother, Edie and I went to vespers at St Rémy, where with great pomp and ceremony they celebrated the Fête des tous Saints. It really was very grand, the church one blaze of light, 300 candles on the high altar, and one organ answering the other, till the beautiful music almost transported one out of oneself, whilst the heavy odour of incense floating through the whole building, imparted a sense of indefinable voluptuousness, perfectly impossible to describe. I had a prayer book in my hand but I don't think I used it much, it seemed so natural in that deliciously enervating atmosphere, to throw aside all reticences and to say just what was in the heart, instead of what on the printed pages was meant for thousands besides yourself. Then we had a grand sermon ¾ of an hour, though it only seemed ten minutes: on love: I defy the french ever to keep that out of the pulpit. L'Abbé Ansault, such an eager impassioned-looking young man, warmed to the congenial subject in no time, and gave us such an eloquent description of our aspirations after eternal happiness and felicity as Bossuet himself could scarcely have done. While he described in language that irresistibly carried his hearers with him, the miseries of death and separation et l'attente, there was scarcely a dry eye in the church and you might have heard his audience sob; I bore up against the general emotion as heroically as he did himself, not because I didn't feel what he was saying, but because I was too interested in it to have any time to cry.

Wed 3rd Nov

A merveille! A Leigh letter arrived tonight to say the shooting is arranged as before: so we shall have our London visit at the right time too, after all. Quelle chance! and if this should be the turning of fortune's tide — but that would be too good to be true; only let me manage London and I daren't even expect any more.

Thank Heavens Lansdowne was married this morning at Westminster Abbey with all imaginary [*sic*] pomp and ceremony: so short of little Lady Maud [Hamilton] coming to an untimely end over her first baby, which the Lord forfend, I may confidently reckon on not hearing that I am engaged to him any longer. It appears that a certain Mr Rann [?] is taking infinite pains to propagate all through London how the scandal of Dieppe is that we went off in a yacht with two Belgians, and for a month or more lived pretty contentedly there: one of the most harmonious Agapemones the 19th century has yet witnessed! It's high time, I perceive, for me to be in England, to contradict such infamous assertions. Attends un peu, M Rann! I have put you down in the debtors' book for that pleasing invention, and sooner or later you will pay me for it.

> *Agapemone*: "love abode". The dictionary adds: "usually with sinister implication". A religious community with this name was founded near Bridgwater, Somerset, in 1849. The "spiritual marriages" were suspected of not always being so. The members lived on a common fund, but got into trouble with authority for "licentious conduct", being popularly supposed to believe in free love.

Saturday 20th November

My last entry made for a very long time in my little room. We start for England tomorrow, and I should like to sit over the fire with you my book for another hour, speculating on how that visit will turn out, but resisting the temptation, castle-building being entirely against my code of morals, besides 8 o'clock tomorrow must see me astir.

Sun 21 Nov

I wonder if there is one single place on earth in which poor humanity appears to greater disadvantage than on board a steam-boat, when it's blowing a little fresh and the white horses are tossing their manes merrily ahead! Such faces as were round me today, and the surprising part is that those who paid the tribute stern nature demanded, scarcely looked as bad as those who sat and meekly bore their fate. One thing I am certain of, that day I felt so very miserable on board the Sea Bird, my expression in no wise resembled theirs, or F——would never have been so lavish in his petits soins. A very nice man Father called "Tommy Trafford" replaced him today, and kept us alive with stories till about 7½ we reached London. I pass over Jeanne's greetings at seeing me, on paper they are stupid things, besides I had too bad a headache to appreciate them. Next day of course I wrote a round robin of letters to divers friends, including as stiff and disagreeable a one to M—— as the most strait-laced of prudes could have dictated. Then Monday wore wearily away, Tuesday like unto it, and Wednesday the answer came. "Dear Miss Miles, I have just received your letter and hasten to answer. I have been in London ever since I wrote to Mrs Miles, laid up from an accident. At present I am unable to leave the house, and as my right fore-finger was dissected by a surgeon yesterday, writing is slow work, so please excuse more from your humble servant, M——. I hope to be able to get to Charles Street some day before you leave."

We had just returned from a round of stupid Kensington visits, coming into the hall first, I saw my letter, slipped it in my muff and so was able to master its contents alone, without two inquisitive eyes following every expression of my face. The sort of feeling that came over me I never experienced before, a choking in the throat, giddy faintness, all mastered and swallowed up in an intense longing to see him if only for a moment, my poor d——! Zéphine came into the room without my noticing and her voice broke in on this meditation. "Madame has sent up to say Sir Fred des Voeux and M Caumont de la Force are in the drawing room. Madame requests Mlle will come down at once." Go down, and talk to those two inane young loungers, when I felt that at the very first word I must irresistibly burst into tears: still somehow or other I must get through it, and I answered calmly, "I require nothing more at present Zéphine, you may go." Then when she had left the room I caught up a pen and scribbled; "Wed, 5½. I have this moment come in and got your letter which pained me more than I can tell. Poor dear thing! And to think of my writing you such an odious letter when you were suffering, being pulled about by doctors — it was too brutal! Don't hurt yourself going out before you can stand it, though I should be so glad to see you, and hear how your accident took place, of course through that hunting or shooting — bah! I hate their very names. Your sincere friend, Alice."

Then I went down and talked nonsense to Fred and other men coming in later, laughed and chaffed and grew quite brilliant — it is the history of all the week, for I never saw him and only heard that he was better once: I dare not send oftener, for after all, what matter is it to me? Yes! that is the cruellest part of all: what matter? I have not the faintest right to interest myself in his well or evil doing, if he were to die tomorrow, it could be no affair of mine — and yet! oh dear, don't let me write any more.

Lord Dupplin comes to see me constantly. He really is a sweet little thing, in his diminutive way, coaxing and insinuating to a degree some people I dare say would vastly prefer him to Mr——, Why can't I! Oh why can't I!

Tues 30 Nov

Went to Broke. The french ambassador La Vallette, Caumont, old Ferguson and ourselves. Of course there being no object of interest to keep the cold out of our bones, the result was what might have been expected in a house where none of the doors or windows shut and mysterious draughts are constantly prevailing: we all got bronchitis and remained in bed. The Tuesday following I was just well enough to return to London. From then till today Friday, nothing. Stuart Hobhouse comes to see me every day and makes desperate love for about 2 hours, in the dullest possible fashion. I support him, as Colonel Martyn has promised me the most magnificent bracelet if I succeed in taking him away from Mrs Shafto, which liaison he disapproves of. Got a very sweet letter from Duppy this morning, inclosing the prettiest photo, and filled with an account of the gay doings at the Duke of Marlborough's. Dear old Alfred Montgomery has just gone: having spent 2 hours solely in sounding M—— 's praises. He declares he's the handsomest and best fellow he ever met. It wasn't politic, I know, but I couldn't help agreeing with him and saying so.

Sat 11th December

A lot of stupid people dined, whether it was them or the sight of all the grand food I couldn't touch I don't know, but towards 9½ n'y tenant plus, my overwrought nerves found relief in the following note despatched to M—— "If you don't come soon, you won't see me at all, as I leave for Leigh Tuesday to vegetate 6 months between trees and my grandfather. I am perfectly convinced you are well enough; people always are, to do what they choose. Anyway you are to come tomorrow whether you faint on the road or not. What bores men are to be sure, to require so much ordering! Yours, Alice." Went to bed with the pleasant reflection that if that peremptory epistle don't bring him, nothing will, and went to sleep preparing a lecture for him and dreamt that he came and I unaccountably relented.

Sunday 12 Dec

Stood for 2 mortal hours looking out of the window with Jeanne, whose sympathy was really the only thing that kept me up. We saw a great many cabs, hansoms, dirty children, cats and churchgoers; Mrs Bruton opposite − but nothing else. At about 3 o'clock Mother departed for Mass with Josephine, she said. I wonder if she knew how grateful I was to her. Then I laid [sic] down on the sofa, and Jeanne read me "Jinny's three balls" a pathetic little story with a brute for a hero. I declared M—— was as bad if not worse, Jeanne said he wasn't, I persisted, she contradicted, until the door opened, and the gentleman in question walking in, put an end to the discussion, closing it all in his favour. Poor fellow, he is so much changed, so ill and wearied, he looks 10 years older than he did in the summer. That didn't prevent me, though, giving him such a lecture, as I flatter myself he never had before. "I knew I was going to catch it," he said ruefully "but I didn't expect anything like this," and in very deed he just about did get all he deserved, which is saying something: Alice, ma petite, je suis contente de toi.[1] "You grow prettier and prettier every day," he told me, with one of his most deliciously appropriative looks. I remarked also with inward satisfaction that he carries my photo about with him: I gave him two more as a reward, which makes four in all: quite a collection. Of course I issued a "not at home" the moment he arrived, and Jeanne saw to it being carried out. Mother was frantic, seeing that I thus sent away about three of her admirers. I wouldn't tell her, either, anything he said, though she cross-questioned me conscientiously: I shan't even say any more to you my book: some things one doesn't want any memoranda to remember, and are altogether too sacred to be talked or written about. I need only say it was a very happy Sunday.

[1]Alice, ma petite . . . . : Alice my girl, I'm pleased with you.

Monday 13th Dec

Went and lunched with Mrs Bramston, who has the most cocotte little house imaginable, all knick-knacks, Dresden, Sèvres and blue ribbon. We talked and laughed a good deal with a handsome young baronet in the Scots Fusiliers and drove afterwards, but I was in at 4½ for M—— and sent away my pet Sir Fred, in case he should arrive and find him. I can't give our interview, for I should cry again, and I have cried far too much over it already. Deprived of all his sweet looks and petting, the result stands out with lamentable clearness: during his father's lifetime, he never can or will have more than £500 a year, and on that sum it is perfectly impossible to marry: so there is an end of it all: and yet even knowing that I cannot, will not give him up, life without him doesn't seem worth having. There let me shut my book up: I don't want to reason or argue: there are some miseries that when you look them boldly in the face, only seem to get instead of clear, more hopelessly embrouillé and perplexing.

Tuesday 14th December — Leigh Court

Arrived here in time for dinner, in what frame of mind you can easily imagine. Kept up with the greatest difficulty, while I was downstairs, and then cried myself to sleep over M—— and woke next morning with just as bad a heart-ache and a head-ache into the bargain.

> Poor Alice — the reason for her self-exile at Leigh being snatched away just as the lugubrious experience begins! And one cannot help wondering which of them decided that marriage on £500 a year was impossible. Did Morland Hutton plead poverty to extricate himself from an engagement to a girl who, whatever her charms and however fond he had become of her, seemed to him unsuitable as a wife? Alice has mentioned an obliging father ready to move out on his son's marriage, as well as a fearsome mother: surely if Hutton had really wanted to marry her he could, if determined enough, have got his way. As it turned out he married Eustacie Arkwright in August 1870.

Sunday 19th December

Well, I am beginning to settle down a little into this vegetable existence: but oh it is such weary work! Willie Davie is my only consolation a lovely boy of six, with eyes so like M—— I sometimes think it is him looking at me again. Of course, the child is devoted to me, as indeed he ought to be, seeing [that] through that resemblance he reigns over me, almost as despotically as the other might. Every evening he comes up to my room, I take him on my knee and tell him stories, which he listens to with rapt attention, looking at me oh so earnestly with M—— 's eyes. "How you do let Willie worry you, I never thought you were so fond of children," his mother said to me the other day. If she could have read my motives, she would have been edified! Don't you think so, mon livre?

Today I was taken to church which of course was very proper and I have nothing to say against it only as the sacred edifice was very dark and the clergyman's voice monotonous in the extreme, insensibly my thoughts began to wander to this time last week; and the idea certainly did suggest itself to me how much better it would be, if M—— 's father would only elect to go where glory awaits him, both for himself and us. The text of the sermon was "for strength is to sit still" — Sit still! Yes, I expect I shall have plenty of that, and of all things to me, inaction is most unbearable. I always think it rusts my faculties instead of resting them: happily though the first encounter knocks off that invariably.

Minnie and Aunt Fanny[1] are here, the latter contemplating a fifth boy and more captious in temper than usual. She steals about the house with woe in her garments and bad temper in her face, a picture of the virtuous British matron who conscious merit makes disdain outward attire; from such a fate at 5 and 30 may a merciful heaven preserve me and mine. As for society, there's not a decent-looking man within a radius of twenty miles. It doesn't much signify, though, for to grandpapa's aged vision his whole sex appears as ravening beasts of prey, always wandering about seeking whom they may destroy: he wouldn't let one into the fold at any price; and I am fully convinced that if a battalion of the Coldstream and Fusiliers were quartered in the village, he'd shut the lodge gates in the guardsmens' faces, and unhesitantly try them at the next Assizes for poaching, if one or two were found admiring the beauties of nature in the grounds.

---

[1]Alice's father's sister, Frances Ferguson Davie. Willie Davie, the little boy with eyes like Morland's, would be her son.

Every Girl's Duty

Xmas Day

I wonder just why because it happens to be the 25th of December people should dress up the church like a merry Andrew,[1] be inflicted with all the children's society at dinner, and invoke impossible blessings they know will never come to pass on each others' heads? Oysters[2] and a £5 note from Grandpapa, accompanied by a sermonising letter respecting my duties as a Xtian woman, is what the day reserved for me. The £5 was of course acceptable, but on the whole I don't know but what I appreciated the oysters most of the three. Charlie has come to enliven us for a little, he is a very nice gentlemanly young fellow indeed, and a sensible relief after such a series of frightful women, we loiter about the conservatory together, sit and chat in the little dining room, and make the most of each other in every possible way. Jeanne sent me the sweetest little leather frame with the remark "Of course I mean it for the photo, to carry about in your pocket, and put under your pillow (if you have arrived at that stage yet!) I thought it would not remain long in your album." Really that child's perspicacity far outstrips her sixteen years! I wrote and thanked her for it adding, "I am very glad you don't think that queer church incident unlucky. Of course I shan't go and see them married as you advise not: I have seen the happy pair though, the bridegroom is a very decent looking young fellow of 8 and 20, but the bride!!! Dear Jeanne, endow a barrel with vitality, surmount it with a countenance whose nose irresistibly reminds one of port wine, throw 6 and 40 summers on this graceful head, and you have as correct a picture as I can draw of Sarah Robinson, the future Mrs H——!! Winter seems a grand time for the old ones getting off, for the night of my arrival I was greeted with the news of Terry Buller's marriage to a man with £4,000 a year. Terry is an excellent damsel of 8 and 30, whose plainness is only equalled by her virtue (for which it perhaps accounts!) for I shrewdly suspect she is one of the many, who were they truthful might give the answer Gertrude did when I was praising one day her stainless morality 'My dear, I don't deserve so much credit, no man ever asked me to be anything else'. 'Enter not into temptation' we pray, 'but deliver us from evil' yet I don't know that I should particularly care about being delivered from temptations of that sort."

[1] A buffoon or jester.
[2] Presumably served at dinner, not given as a present.

Tuesday 28th December

Charlie and my Darling Boy left, I don't know how ever I should have got over it, if the sweetest letter from "Baby Dupplin" full of regret at not having seen me before we left London, had not come to console me, under the double affliction. Here is my answer, sent some days later: "Thanks for your very pretty letter, though it was full of fibs, as you knew quite well we were in London when you returned from Blenheim, and so far from being away shooting were seen by I don't know how many men at the club, and by Mrs Bramston with a lot of women at the opera. In fact she intended to ask you to come to lunch one day when I did, only I thought your conduct unworthy of such a pleasure, and we had a charming young Sir Wm Somebody of the Fusiliers instead."

I wonder what he will think of that, his pretty little Babyship!

Tuesday December 31st

I am sitting very quietly in my room, having escaped from the nonentities below, my photo beside me, and feel irresistibly impelled to write a few words here, for the last time this year: poor old '69, they are ringing him out very merrily, and though I suppose I ought to try and be sentimental over his decease, I don't think I regret him much. It has not been an unhappy year for me, far from it, there has been plenty of pleasure, a good deal of downright excitement, but of real happiness only those five London days:[1] on the whole, I suppose I ought not to complain, the balance is a fair one: 1870 will not hold 5 whole days happiness for me I fear, I have so very little faith in the future: who knows, perhaps this time 12 months, I may not even think the same, and yet, and yet — I don't believe in that way I shall change — but it is getting late, let me close my book, and end that old year at least with his name. Goodnight M——!

[1]These must be the days in July when she went to Hampton Court with Morland Hutton.

So ended 1869, and Alice's own words are the best for her feelings. She was nineteen, and had lost the man who had aroused the most worthy and tender emotion she had experienced for any: the man who might, by his honesty, integrity and intelligence, have made a husband she could have loved and respected. But, typically, she picked herself up and began to look around for new opportunities.

Having landed herself in the puritanical atmosphere of Leigh Court, she could amuse herself only by "being naughty", as she called it, whenever she got the chance. She jumped at a visit to Aunt Pamela, of whom she was fond, and had a pleasant week in spite of the astringent presence of an "antiquated virgin . . . a combination of bones, beak and malice". She then removed to Kings Weston, where others of her father's family lived, and met an uncle by marriage, Pat McDonall, who had "the spice of a sinner" about him. Their instant friendship, private jokes and habit of disappearing together when out hunting, infuriated his wife, Aunt Addy (or Adsa). (Alice, by the way, seems to have acquitted herself well in the hunting field, although she has made only one passing reference to riding in her diary.) When her grandfather lent her a heavy theological tome for the good of her soul, Alice astutely passed it on to Pat so that he could digest it for her. This caused a "charming row" when her grandfather discovered it: he declared her to be the "greatest hypocrite of his acquaintance".

The best entertainment was provided by a newly discovered "cousin", Willy Kington, Captain in Her Majesty's 4th Hussars. They hit it off and Alice immediately brought all her weapons to bear on Willy, reducing him to dog-like devotion and causing a great rumpus in the family by thus playing with the poor boy's feelings. When he had to set sail for India she saw him go without a moment's regret. His farewell letter wished her "every happiness, darling, an obedient spouse with lots of money, and a safe deliverance (as the prayerbook hath it) from Leigh". He had come to understand her well. She read all his letters over once more, then burnt them. "And so ended that little episode, gone in that flicker of fire — ah well, tout passe, tout casse, tout lasse, dans cette vie! Flirtation, like all the rest, is only temporary and this one is dead and gone."

Her comment on one of her conversations with the attractive Uncle Pat (perhaps embellished in retrospect) is interesting. She says:

> "I don't think I ever experienced that indefinable drawing of one
> intellect towards another the French call sympathie, so strongly

before: a feeling utterly devoid of the pleasurable excitement or
ennui of flirtation. Stronger, different, the dawning, I suppose of
that friendship I have been a little apt to scoff at, as existing
between a young and beautiful woman and any impressionable
man; but which I could inspire and reciprocate in Pat, if only
they would let us, which they won't."

Pat commented on her conduct and character, likening her to Mary
Stuart (which must have pleased her) and was intrigued by her habit
of spending so much of her leisure time writing. He told her that he
had such faith in her abilities that he was sure — without ever having
seen a page — that if she chose to publish she would meet with
success. Alice made an ambiguous reply, then added: "I wouldn't do it
for the whole world. What is money and a name to a woman, when
compared to her future? To make a book really interesting you must
describe daring passions no man would care that his wife should have
experienced . . . Oh, Uncle Pat, don't YOU understand?" Which, it
seems, he did, commending her commonsense in resisting the temptations of fame and fortune in the interests of respectability.

Perhaps Alice had read too many French novels. Obviously she
thought publicity equalled notoriety and would undermine her other
ambition of making a "good" marriage. Not until seven years after
this conversation, when she was a safely established matron, did Alice
dare to attempt to get a toe in the door of literature: and even then she
hid behind a masculine pseudonym.

PART TWO

Afterwards

The Squire's Lady

THE spring of 1870 found Alice back in Paris, deep in her usual round of boring balls and charming dinners with handsome specimens of "the genus detrimental". But not for long. The Franco-Prussian war broke out and most of the British, including the Mileses, left in a hurry. The horrific siege of Paris began that September, its starvation and misery lasting until the city's surrender in January 1871. The Empress Eugénie fled to England, soon to be joined by the ailing Napoleon III. The Second Empire came to an end.

It is possible that Alice found the war a blessing in disguise, because she would have arrived in London in time to catch the end of the Season − unless, of course, she was buried down at Leigh. Her diaries have ended, so we cannot tell. But we do know, from later evidence, that she was at Cowes Week, which is held in August. And there she met the dark stranger who figures in this report from *The Times* in December 1870.

St George's Hanover Square was, last Saturday, 17th December, thronged with fair spectators to witness the nuptials of Mr George Duppa, who has amassed a colossal fortune in New Zealand, and Miss Miles, grand daughter of Sir William Miles, of Leigh Court, near Bristol. The bridegroom, said to be three and thirty years older than his fair bride, arrived at about half-past eleven, with his best man Mr Bullar. The beautiful bride was dressed in magnificent Spanish lace, over the richest grosgrain silk, a small spray of orange flowers and myrtle in her hair and a long tulle veil. She wore splendid diamond ornaments, the gift of Mr Duppa, and carried a most magnificent scent-bottle. There were six bridesmaids, dressed in white muslin trimmed with Valenciennes insertion over pink, white bonnets

151

with small bunches of pink roses, and long tulle veils. They each wore a gold locket with a monogram of turquoise and pearls, presented to them by the bridegroom. After the breakfast at 18 Bolton Street, the happy couple left for Eastbourne where they will spend the honeymoon. Mrs Duppa's travelling dress was composed of groseille[2]-coloured cashmere over a satin petticoat of the same colour. The bride had numberless presents, and those in jewellery were of the most costly description. Amongst the company at the breakfast, conspicuous for her graceful beauty and youthful appearance, was Mrs Miles, the mother of the bride, whose dress was of Rose du Barry silk trimmed with Brussels lace looped with black velvet, and she wore a very pretty bonnet of white chip, with pink feathers.

How did this marriage come about, just six months after Alice's last entry in her Parisian diary? Her bridegroom had no coronet, no title, and was not even the heir to a baronetcy. What he *did* have was a large estate in Kent, an immense fortune, and thirty-three years' seniority over his bride.

Elwyn Evans has written much about the Duppa family, which he has extensively researched, and the following note has kindly been provided by him:

George Duppa was the youngest son of a large family, and he sailed for New Zealand in 1839. There he amassed a large fortune before he returned to England in 1864. He opened up several large sheep-rearing runs, claimed to be the first to export wool to England, and was one of the first settlers actually to make a fortune in New Zealand. He was remembered there with little affection, for his business methods were ruthless; he took no part in civic affairs; he made no secret of the fact that his sole ambition was to return to England a rich man and settle down to his rightful role of an English country gentleman. This he did successfully. By the early 1870s he had purchased much of the Duppa family's estates, and from their marriage he and Alice became the occupants of Hollingbourne House, in Hollingbourne, a village near Maidstone, in Kent, although he did not

---

[1] A *groseille à grappe* is a redcurrant; a *groseille noire* is a black currant; a *groseille verte* is a gooseberry. When we imagine the colour of this cashmere we can take our pick.

fully become the owner of the Hollingbourne estate until pro-tracted Chancery actions became completed in 1881.

George Duppa's character and his later years will be further revealed as Alice's story unfolds.

Why Alice married when and whom she did can only be conjec-tured. There would have been pressure on her to marry, and marry "well". Three sisters were growing up close behind her, and while her grandfather lived her father was — or felt himself to be — short of money. She herself had expensive tastes which she could not hope to gratify except as a rich man's wife. Alice as a spinster — one of those unfortunate beings about whom she was so unkind — was unthink-able. Alice as a marchioness would have been more like it, but she was a remarkably realistic girl in her way, and her experience of society had probably taught her that while grand young men were happy to flirt with penniless beauties who had naughty mothers, they were most unlikely to marry them. With Morland Hutton she had allowed herself to play with the idea of life in a cottage (a pretty well-furnished one); but the passage in her diary where she does this suggests that she felt herself to be giving way to a weakness rather than opting for the right course. The evidence points to her agreeing with the society which had produced her, and genuinely believing that it was her duty — and not a disagreeable duty, either — to marry money.

In addition to this, she was becoming bored with the pattern of her life in Paris and London, and miserably uncomfortable about her mother and "Tartuffe". It was only eight months earlier that she had written in her diary: "I don't know with what dominant feeling most girls begin their married life, but am perfectly convinced that mine will be gratitude, for emancipation from present evil!" (She was not to know — who *does* know, while still in their teens? — how very like her parent she would eventually prove to be.) George Duppa was old enough to be her father, certainly; but he could give her respectability, as well as lots of money and an interesting change. And to give him his due he was not an unattractive man.

His photograph shows him as handsome in a darkling way, and although he appears to have been ruthless as a speculator, unscrupu-lous as an employer and unpopular as a settler, he may have had charm. As a yachtsman he was both daring and successful, and the *Encyclopedia of New Zealand* describes him as "able, energetic, well-spoken, well-connected and goodlooking . . . he was musical and could sing well, and was a splendid horseman who could ride a race in a finished style." All this could have made him quite a gratifying conquest to a nineteen-year-old girl, and the rest of the *Encyclopedia*'s portrait — "self-confident, crudely selfish . . . [and] unscrupulous" would not have appeared at once. And could not the same have been said of Alice? Perhaps they deserved each other. At any rate, barely four months after their meeting at Cowes, they married.

In her diary (see pages 97 and 100) Alice had speculated that it might be possible to enjoy the role of wife, mother and Lady Bountiful. Now that role was hers. In June 1871 she was brought by her husband to his family home at Hollingbourne in Kent, to the welcoming sound of the church bells.

Hollingbourne was, and still to a large extent is, in two settlements. The upper village, at the foot of the North Downs, is a single street of houses ranging in date from the fifteenth to the twentieth century. The church is here, and so is the mill pond, the mill with its wheel, and the sources of the "bourne" (stream) which gives the village half its name. To the south, down an ancient winding road, is the lower village, equally old but now including the railway and the Board School, both of which originated during Alice's married life there. The Duppas' house, a severely classical building of about 1800, is high up on Hollingbourne Hill and commands a view southwards to the village farms, and beyond them to the Weald and the Greensand Ridge.

This was to be Alice's domain for the next sixteen years. Only a few extracts have survived from the diaries she kept after her marriage, but she flits in and out of that kept by another great lady of the village, Mrs Louisa Thomas, who was old enough to be Alice's grandmother and found the young bride beautiful and gracious. She pens little vignettes of Alice, mentioning Mrs Duppa's beauty; the expensive medical man called to her first confinement; the silk and lace she wore at christenings; the two fine babies who accompanied her on a call. She shows us Alice painting on china and Alice sitting on a haystack, and she records the dinners, suppers and tea-drinkings shared by the two families.

Alice's own voice is heard again, although only from time to time and obliquely, in the notebooks she kept of her personal accounts. Here there are records of flannel, rabbits, waistcoats and jellies bestowed on the poor, and readings to the sick. Sometimes Alice's ironic humour asserts itself, yet there is genuine pleasure too, in the people's gratitude to her; and perhaps the sheer novelty of altruism appealed to her.

January 1st 1875 Walked down to the village. Took Mrs Glover Bryan's old knitted jacket for little Emily, undressed her and put it on. Poor little thing, she had been suffering from cold and diarrhoea. Mrs Sage in her bedroom looking very triste dressing the twelfth baby, the tiniest little fright I ever beheld. Left her two orders for meat 2 lbs at 9d a pound while I'm away, also some old blankets as they had none.

January 2nd Read to Mrs Jenner, gave her a rabbit. Poor old dear, she is always so grateful for the smallest mercies in the shape of my august presence. To Mrs Atkins I gave the lovely quilt I made last night as she had the most awful cough and no bedclothes to cover her.

February 5th Found Mrs Sage wonderfully well, gave her 1 yd flannel for the baby, who has grown quite pretty.

Feb 7th Dear old Mrs Jenner; sat and read to her for half an hour. Her patience under her sufferings is wonderful; she told me today she was sure all trials were for some wise end: if only one could think so!

Feb 27th Grace Taylor in the last stages of consumption, poor thing. Took her half a dozen oranges and half lb arrowroot . . . Poor thing, she looks so wan and lovely.

23rd March For the last week I have been nearly every day to sit with Grace. I was there at half past one and at ten she died peacefully and begging her parents to give up their evil ways and join her where she was going.

24 March Went and took our last look of Grace so still now and peaceful after all her troubles. They had dressed her all in white and draped the bed with white: calm as she looked it haunted me for days afterwards. Death is so fearful to life: even in its fairest aspects.

Similar notes continue, together with long lists of dinners sent, as well as bottles of port, petticoats, eggs, orders for meat and bread, and her own sons' cast-off clothing. Deplorable as conditions were for the rural poor in winter, Alice, like many others, did what she could — short of changing the system — to alleviate hardship. The recipients were suitably grateful, for most of them still accepted it as God's will that there should be a rich man in his castle and a poor one at his gate: and they called down his blessing on their benefactress.

7 October 1876 I told Mrs Jenner I was going away for a fortnight and she gave me her solemn benediction: "And may peace and happiness go with you m'am. May your children grow up to be a comfort and a glory to you, and may you be spared to the poor and miserable for many and many a year."

31st October Paid Mrs Wood a visit . . . Such a dear old woman in a big white cap and frill . . . she had thirteen children and only two living. "The Lord only lends 'em to us at best, M'am" she told me. Her master's speech (as she calls him) was best of all: "and it's Mrs Duppa who sent all this? Why, what a blessed woman she be!"

13th Jan Took my godchild Alice a picture book, flannel petticoat, two yards blue stuff for a dress, and Archie's grey gilet. Little Alice asks her mother if I am not "quite the greatest, loveliest lady in the world."

Alice's notes, ceasing in 1877, leave a small but vivid picture of the age. It seems that apart from her frequent visits to her family and friends, her village visiting was interrupted only by outbreaks of infectious disease or extremes of weather. There is no evidence that she was anything other than reasonably contented with her rural life. Her first son, Bryan, was born eleven months after her marriage, in November 1871, to be followed by Archie in September 1873. In the same year her mother produced a son, Cecil, and one would like to know what comment passed between mother and daughter. Alice was an affectionate mother, though like all women of her class and time she was content to leave her children in the care of servants for lengthy periods; and like all wives of gentlemen must frequently have been left to her own devices, while her husband was about the important business of making money, shooting, and sitting on the magistrates' bench. Her account books throw glimmers of light on some of her solitary activities, for she mentions small sums gained from chickens, the sale of puppies, and painting on china. There are references too, to cheques "from Geo" and from her parents. She was a free spender on her trips to London, it seems, but how generous George was in his allowances to her remains in question. He became involved in heavy expenditure on his estates after his marriage, and found need to economise.

A rich husband, children, pleasant rural surroundings, a big house with plenty of servants, visits to London, pastimes like sketching, and useful occupations like looking after the poor: the pattern of Alice's life was repeated in thousands of homes throughout the country. What more could any well-brought up gentlewoman want?

But Alice did want more. Her energy and appetite for admiration were undiminished by her marriage, and in its first decade she began to write essays (perhaps encouraged by Tommy Bowles) and a mountain of verbiage in the form of notes and fair copies of sermons. The two activities make a piquant contrast.

A few of the sermons were those preached by H. Montague Villiers at All Saints, Clifton, the church she attended when staying with her grandfather; but the majority were given by the Rev. George H. Wilkinson at St Peter's, Eaton Square, London, in the very heartland of fashionable society. They were very long, eloquent and carefully planned — and to modern taste, dreadfully boring. In the 1870s volumes of sermons were popular, being suitable reading for a Sunday evening (especially if one had not felt "equal" to church that morning), and for reading aloud (as Alice sometimes did) to the hapless poor. But it still seems extraordinary that a young woman as frivolous as Alice, daughter of a mother as frivolous as Lady Miles, should have put in all this hard labour. It suggests that she was trying very very hard to be what she ought to be.

It is therefore something of a shock to turn to her own writings of the period: the essays entitled "Constancy", "Blue Roses", "Dram Drinking", "Beauty and the Beast", "Women of the Day", "Humbug", "Drifting", "Duty versus Inclination", "Martyrs" and "Flirtation". In all of them she conceals herself behind a male persona, presumably because she was aiming to get into print — as she did, with "Flirtation", which follows.

FLIRTATION.

Who was it that described flirtation as the "preliminary canter to love-making"? It was a witty definition of an undefinable thing, and yet, in one way, fell wide of the mark. Flirtation, *pur et simple*, as practised by an adept in the art, contains no elements of the tender passion. Once arouse that, and all the telling artillery of looks and smiles goes down before a tyrant, whose unhappy peculiarity consists in always presenting us at our worst when we most desire to please. Flirtation has none of these drawbacks. Born of indolence, wafted hither and thither on every breath of caprice, fostered on vanity, and also that desire to please that — bless them for it! — is so striking a characteristic of the feebler sex, it offers a most fascinating pastime to the upper classes. I exempt the people from it without a moment's hesitation; the uncouth jests, the clumsy adoration that is current among them cannot be dignified by the name of flirtation. When some fair rustic by chance can wield the delicate weapon, she invariably forsakes her kindred and her father's house, to take a doubtful place, *à la main gauche*, among her betters. Flirtation may almost entirely be said to consist in the science of implication, and it is incredible to what perfection it can be carried. In my youth I enjoyed the honour of being personally acquainted with one of the greatest coquettes our country ever produced. I attacked the enemy with my eyes open. I tried to analyse her method, but in vain! The fascinations half Europe had succumbed to were too much for me. When I emerged bleeding from the conquest, I only carried away with me a hazy idea of eyes veiled by long lashes, that at a given moment in your discourse would lift themselves and dwell on you till you stammered and forgot your sentence under their magnetic light; of lips that framed the most indifferent sentences, as if her audience was the only one in the whole world fitted to understand and sympathise; of a soft white hand whose slightest touch was a caress. Certainly this lady had beauty, such as rarely falls to her sisters' lot to aid her in her crusade against the peace of mind of her fellow-creatures, but I have seen the same result attained by comparatively ugly women. Perfect tact, an indomitable desire of power, coupled with perfect indifference as to what the result of this pastime may be on the future lives of her victims, may be looked on as excellent substitutes for charms that it rests with Providence alone to give or withold. Your practised coquette relies mostly on herself, and finds herself all-sufficient. You will remark that all I have written applies exclusively to the fairer sex. I do not wish even to mention such a despicable creature as the male flirt must always be in the eyes of any right-thinking person.

In their position of the sought and not the seekers, these coquetries are women's natural right. Remember, also, they are generally directed against men older, and therefore it is presumed, more experienced than themselves.

The Lord of Creation, whose proud prerogative it is to throw the handkerchief, need descend to no such wiles.

FLORIAN

The above is the edited version which appeared in *Vanity Fair* on April 15th 1876. It is shorter by almost half than Alice's original. The young woman who wrote it seems a great deal nearer the girl of the diaries who prided herself on the artistry with which she subjugated guards officers than she is to flannel-bestowing, sermon-reading Mrs Duppa.

The tone of that essay is the only hint left us by Alice herself of events which surfaced eleven years later, on September 28th 1887, in the diary of Mrs Louisa Thomas: "Everyone is talking of the Duppa affair, but no one knows what it is." And on that same day her daughter Mary wrote: "Poor Mrs Duppa went to London by train with luggage, saying she never meant to return."

The account of "the Duppa affair" which follows, has been pieced together from legal papers, the extracts from diaries mentioned on page 160 (which were copied from lost originals by a solicitor's clerk), letters from Alice to George, and several statements made by him including a detailed deposition to his solicitor. All these documents were in the boxes made available by Mrs Newbury.

'The Duppa Affair'

GEORGE'S story of their marriage, set out in his statement in support of his petition for divorce, offers evidence that there were flaws in the partnership from the first; but for at least the first ten years there were no outward signs of this. He recounts how in August 1870 he had met for the first time the Mileses and their three daughters, at Cowes "whither they had come from Paris on the breaking up of the Empire". He had heard of Alice's beauty, and found her the most lovely girl he had ever met – and was pounced on by her mother as a husband for her. "There was a sort of half-engagement," the acquaintance continued in London and they were married in December. After a short time at Eastbourne, they went to Leamington for the winter, where Mrs Duppa "used to kick me in the night, saying it was in her sleep". Presently he felt obliged to move into a separate room.

Once they were settled in Hollingbourne House, he would go out to his farm or on other business after breakfast and they would not meet till five o'clock tea. "She always estranged herself from me from the first . . . was on indifferent, cool and distant terms . . . nothing would have afforded me so much pleasure as to be on affectionate and confidential terms with my wife, but she would not."

In retrospect, the first hint of impending disaster may have come in 1881. During the years 1881 to 1887 Alice frequently visited not only Leigh Court, but also London, to see her parents, sisters and friends – often without George. Solicitors later acting for George obtained some of her diaries for those years, and extracts were copied by clerks, to be used in evidence. She had given up taking notes of sermons in about 1879, so perhaps she was cultivating other interests, although she still frequented both the Jesuit church in Farm Street, and the Carmelites in Kensington. In January 1881 Alice received "a sudden telegram from Father summoning me to take care of Mother who is in bed with bad rheumatism". It was suspected that Alice would get her mother to plead illness, giving Alice an excuse to go to London, where she indulged in much visiting, shopping and theatre-going.

Alice spent Christmas 1881 at Leigh Court, George joining her later. A family named Ames was staying there, and "Major Ames painted Mrs Duppa's portrait there in an attic painting room". The Ameses and the Mileses had been acquainted for some years. Alice's diary says Captain Ames was there and they had a "capital ball" and danced till 3 a.m. There were apparently three Ames brothers: Gerard (Major Ames); Victor, who was also a painter; and Ossie (Oswald). All three were in the Army.

Little was recorded of 1882, though much was happening. In July Alice complained of heat "which never agrees with me" and admitted to being miserable and hysterical. It became evident that she was pregnant for the third time. George's calculations of the dates of her absences from home made him suspicious; but when he put it to her she "laughed it off. She is an extraordinary woman and laughs anything off." (How this echoes some of those early diary entries when she "laughed merrily" at the discomfort of some hapless male!)

The child, Alice's third son, was born on January 14th 1883 and was christened Berridge Greville George. George states: "I did not feel sure that I was the father . . . [but] things went on as before." After Berridge's birth, "I shortly afterwards ceased cohabitation . . . I found myself too much affected by imagination of the possible adulterous intercourse"; also "If I did not touch her . . . any other child she might have must necessarily belong to some other person. I never afterwards resumed cohabitation." As time went on "I gradually dropped her . . . I never kissed her or took her into dinner . . . we continued to have meals together. I did not do anything to set the servants speculating."

George makes no reference to another event of 1883. The couple's second son Archie was now aged nine, and judging by his photographs, was a handsome and intelligent child, dark like his father. He became suddenly ill, and after a few weeks of suffering, died of "meningitis and exhaustion", on March 19th. This tragedy, which might have been expected to draw George and Alice together, did not seem to do so, and by May Alice was again shopping and visiting in London.

The death of Archie was the more poignant because their first son, Bryan, seems to have been far less intelligent, though affectionate and good, and was something of a disappointment to his parents. He had been placed at Oundle School, but late in May 1883, Alice, without George, visited his housemaster to talk about Bryan, now aged eleven and a half. In the train returning to London, Alice wrote George one of the most simple and sincere, and therefore touching, of her surviving letters.

The train

Dearest Peter[1]

I can only tell you it is really fortunate that I came down to Oundle. So far from my being an unsettling influence Mr H said it would give Bryan extra status in his house, and that personally he was never so thankful to see anyone in his life, as there was much he wished to say about B that he could not write. We had what to me was a most painful conversation and he will write to you on Sat. when I am there to explain every point of his letter, and to tell you the only conditions on which he can consent to keep the child, who remember, is no wise naughty but in many ways naturally deficient. Alas! alas! for my beautiful clever dead darling, who would have been beloved by all and such a credit to us.

There was a dear little lad there so like him that it brought the tears to my eyes. He slept in Bryan's room and I tucked him up too and hugged him when he was in bed for the sake of my little gathered flower in heaven.

Mrs Hansell was most kind and made me quite at home, indeed I was delighted with both her and her husband, and consider we are most fortunate in having discovered anyone like them to take charge of our anxiety. Dear Boy, he was so affectionate too and glad to see me, and sent you any amount of love and kisses . . . I feel too miserable about both children, the lost and the living.

Your loving Pearl

Archie's photographic portrait may be seen in his Italianate memorial in Hollingbourne Church.

Whatever feelings the couple might have shared, George makes no reference to them in his continued statement. It was their habit at first to write very frequently when they were apart. He kept all her letters

[1]"Peter" was her nickname for George; he called her "Pearl".

but "Mrs Duppa does not keep letters . . . I used to commence 'Dearest Pearl' or 'Dearest Alice' but [later] nothing more affectionate than 'Dear Alice' not even 'My dear Alice.' "

In January 1884 Leigh Court was electrified by a visit of the Prince of Wales, to shoot the Leigh Court game and to attend a concert at the Colston Hall, organised by Lady Miles in aid of the local hospital and infirmary. The visit merited a whole page of close print in the Bristol *Times and Mirror*, though the loyal locals were much disappointed at catching the merest glimpse of the Prince. Alice gives her own slant on the event: she was: "attacked by the old parson about the Royal visit, AE[1] not being fortunate enough to meet with his approval." The occasion seems to have been a success – Alice wore white brocade and "AE sat in my pocket as much as etiquette permitted". Shooting in the rain to "gratify the Royal Caprice" was less enthralling, but compensated for by a grand ball, where she wore white satin and violettes. She sat next to AE "who made jokes all the time", and "paced a quadrille with him".

Her sister Mabel's wedding followed in May. The family took it upon themselves to visit her next day, and there was much ribaldry about Mabel's disgracing herself on her wedding night by screaming and fainting – an unedifying morsel which could have come out in the divorce court.

The summer of 1884 passed with holidays in Dover and a touching moment when Alice's favourite boatman wept when he learned of little Archie's death. Alice continued to write frequently to George, as "Peter" and occasionally "Beastie". She writes of the sea, and bathing, and asks him to come down, or to send things for the children, or to look after Fib and Truth, her (significantly named?) dogs. She suffers occasional gastric attacks, sometimes triggered by anxiety. An outbreak of smallpox in Hollingbourne caused her to extend her stay away. She looks forward to seeing George's "black and tan old face". The disasters of the Sudan War (1885) are barely noted, save to observe that the theatres in London are empty. She sometimes professes concern with George's affairs, but her letters are rarely serious and are frequently playful: addressing him as "an odious old person", nonetheless she anticipates with pleasure reunion on his "marital bosom" or in his "appreciative (I hope) arms". His letters must have been less amiable for she asks for "a kind one". "Poor old

[1]AE: Albert Edward, Prince of Wales.

lamb, I hope you are not too dull. Goodbye, dear old fellow, a big kiss." It is hard to believe these letters are written by a cold and faithless wife, as described by George, yet as we know, Alice was capable of writing fiction with apparent sincerity.

"In the summer of 1885 I could tell from Mrs Duppa's figure that she was again enceinte . . . she did not deny . . . I said I should put her in the Divorce Court . . . she said she should destroy herself. I told her she should not add crime to vice. There was very little said . . . I thought a great deal about it."

In August George saw a letter arrive from Lady Miles. Seeking to know what *she* thought of the turn of events, he opened it in Alice's presence and read it to her. Lady Miles's letter describes in mocking terms the *congé* given to one of her own admirers, and encloses his love-lorn missive for Alice's amusement; she continues:

> I suppose your figure tells its own story now. Does George say anything about it? If he adores Berry [Berridge] he will not want to part with him. He is a fine little fellow and looks the soul of honesty and his dad − no-one could take him for an ugly black Duppa. Yours, darling, very lovingly, Mother. You can be confined here if you like, it would be less irritating to your nerves to get rid of Hollingbourne for a while.

One can imagine the unhappy George's feelings on reading this.

He goes on, in his statement, to speak of his own ill-health − a severe chest infection in the winter of 1884−85, and a serious injury to his leg in April 1886. Alice declined to answer what she termed George's "unpleasant questions" about the paternity of her child, and asked why he "shouldn't allow things to go on quietly and comfortably the same as her father and mother did, they were as happy as birds . . . I remarked that her father might submit to be made a cuckold of but I wouldn't."

Before the birth of this fourth child − its paternity still unknown − Alice hinted that as George disapproved of abortion, which she had mentioned, she thought he should accept it as his. The baby, a girl, was born on January 19th 1886. "The same evening she [Alice] took my hand and asked me to forgive her." Not unnaturally George said he could not, nor could he set any credence on her promises to amend her behaviour, and to dismiss her lover, so "she threw my hand aside". The baby, registered by Alice, was christened Vivienne

Muriel. From thenceforward, George's conduct was as cold as possible without actually "kicking her out of the house".

George refused to acknowledge the child, or to enquire further into its origin, or "even its godparents". The nurse "was always thrusting her into my arms" but he would have nothing to do with her. And yet — "as the child grew older she became engaging and I became attached to her — I had to take drives because of my leg and I used to take the child with me and either the nurse or Mrs Duppa." Not the action of a totally cold, cruel or ruthless man.

For a while, all was quiet. George was convinced that sooner or later he would discover the father's name. He was sick, ageing, in pain, and concerned about his financial and farming affairs which were worsening. He noticed sometimes that Mrs Duppa wore diamonds he had not given her; but these and other articles could have been presents from friends or family: as for dresses, she had so many he had no idea which were old or new, and equally no idea which he had paid for. She had an account at Marshall & Snelgrove's, which he paid as required. She continued to visit London — he could see no point in preventing it: "she took the bit between her teeth." "We continued always on speaking terms . . . we never had any words or anything that could enlighten the servants at all — nothing vulgar of that sort . . . she seemed always anxious to kiss me in the presence of servants . . . I used to avoid it . . . she was most marked in her attentions to me as if to impress upon me the great interest she took in me — at the same time that she was making love to another man."

In February 1886 Alice wrote to George from Hollingbourne: "Dearest Geo, many thanks for the cheque, safely received. I do not know why you should make up your mind to treat me like an outcast for the remainder of our lives, it is not for either of our happiness to [?] the rest of our time out, we live together like linked convicts and enough to kill us both. I will not write any more, as my letters are evidently as objectionable to you as myself. Your affectionate, in spite of all, Alice."

In May, referring to their marriage settlement, he must "do as you think fit". This is signed "affectionately, ACD". There are many more extracts of letters among the divorce papers, and a few extracts from Alice's diaries up to 1886; but the letters are not dated by her, though they have dates added in pencil (by George, presumably) and they are a strange mixture of professed affection and anger, with the occasional plea for the continuance of life together.

The last entries from Alice's diaries of December 1886 mention the scandalous "Colin Campbell case" in which Lord Colin Campbell sued his wife, née Gertrude Blood, for divorce, while she cross-petitioned on grounds of cruelty. Lady Miles, who was an older cousin of Lady Colin, was a prime witness in the most sensational divorce case London had seen, and came out of it with no moral halo shining round her own character. Because of the sordid nature of the evidence, no women were permitted to attend, apart from witnesses, but the case was reported in chop-licking detail by the press. Naturally, Alice followed the case in which her mother and cousin were involved with the greatest interest, and when it ended with "Great excitement . . . verdict 'not proved' on both sides" it may have given her some pause for thought about how she herself might react to being dragged through the courts, if George took a mind to do it.

In 1887 an uneasy truce continued, George becoming increasingly ill and morose, Alice still meeting her unknown lover, and perhaps becoming more brazen about her activities. But in September George lighted upon a letter addressed by Alice to Major Gerard Ames, and at last he had the evidence he sought.

On September 6th 1887, Meynell & Pemberton, a firm of solicitors in London, received a request from George for an interview on an urgent and very private matter. On the 18th Alice wrote to Mr Meynell: "For God's sake try and patch up this wretched affair . . . it will kill him if he forces action." But a letter was drafted by the solicitors on the 19th, for George to send to Alice's father, Sir Philip Miles, informing him of "a painful business respecting your daughter Alice" who was being charged with misconduct and "practically did not deny it . . . As she threatened suicide I am unwilling to write my decision while she is alone at Hollingbourne. Perhaps you or some member of your family (other than her mother) could go to her tomorrow . . . and arrange for her leaving . . ."

But something went wrong, for Alice did make an apparent suicide attempt on September 21st by taking chloroform and laudanum, though she soon recovered, and was obliged finally to leave Hollingbourne House for London, taking rooms at 3 Marlborough Mansions in Victoria Street.

Between then and the end of 1887, there accrued a voluminous correspondence and sheaves of memos between Meynell & Pemberton, George Duppa, and other parties. All kinds of effort were made to provide evidence for the allegations made by George, including

Bryan and Archie Duppa

Alice at about the time of her second marriage

*Alice's third and fourth children, Berridge and Vivienne,
and her second husband, Gerard Vivian Ames.*

*". . . the benevolent may
select and receive in a few
hours any article of
clothing suitable for the
most destitute." An
illustration from Pryce
Jones's catalogue, found
among the Duppa papers.*

THE "NIGHTINGALE" BED JACKET (Registered).
Made of Milled Scarlet Flannel, 3/1 each.
GREY CALICO BEDGOWNS, 1/10½ each.   Very acceptable to old women

Alice's beautiful daughters, Vivienne (in the chair) and Eve.
Alice herself has now become "Ma". The photograph of
George Bernard Shaw was taken by one of her family.

shadowing Alice by a private detective, and taking statements from various servants. Alice's solicitors, Lewis & Lewis (which firm included her brother-in-law) made no serious attempt to deny the charges against Alice and Gerard, but tried to defeat George's petition for divorce on the grounds of his condonation and connivance, and his own alleged adultery with a laundry-maid. No sound evidence for the last accusation could be produced.

What *did* weaken George's case very considerably was that although he had suspected Alice of misconduct since 1882 or 1883, it was not until 1887 that he finally acted. His explanation of this dilatoriness, apart from his increasing ill-health, was that he could not guess the identity of the other man, and was under the impression that he could not sue until he could name a co-respondent. But even after he had intercepted letters, discovered the lover's name, and written to Meynell & Pemberton, he still vacillated from time to time, and endangered his whole case by continuing to see Alice.

An episode of black farce occurred at the end of September, when the astonished Mr Meynell was confronted in his office early one morning by both Mr and Mrs Duppa — the latter accusing the lawyer of advising George to petition, which he of course denied, it not being his professional duty either to persuade or dissuade. Mrs Duppa became abusive, and said her husband was so weak she could make him do anything: to prove it she would take him back to Hollingbourne. The next day George managed to return to his solicitors alone, and explained how he had taken refuge in his club, only to be told a lady awaited him in a hansom. She, having already stolen his luggage from the club, "made" him go to Jermyn Street (where he had rooms) and they dined together and passed the night there (George was at pains to explain that he slept in his dressing room, adding he had had no sleep and felt very ill); he arose at 5.30 a.m., and departed to his club with his luggage, and there breakfasted. However, he was not to escape, for Mrs Duppa again appeared and "made" him come to the solicitors. She still planned to take him to Hollingbourne, but the solicitors explained in the most emphatic terms that this would vastly endanger his prospects of a successful petition. George then fled to Brighton and so escaped. He admitted that when Alice "cries and pleads" he could not resist her: "she could do as she liked with him".

Alice had attempted a patched-up reconciliation which had failed; her attempt to cross-petition looked like failing; and her attempt to prejudice his case on grounds of connivance failed. Her final fling was to capture the children (it is not clear which of them). Lady Miles appeared in a fly at Hollingbourne in George's absence, and she — "that animal" as he called her — "intruded herself" and took the children to London.

A long statement was taken by the solicitors from the eldest son, Bryan, now sixteen, who recounted the history of his own acquaintance with Major Ames. It began that Christmas at Leigh Court, but he did not see Ames again until they met at Dover in 1886. Bryan and Alice stayed at Marine Place, while Ames stayed at a hotel, and they would all meet on the beach. Alice would write letters, Ames would sketch, they would all three spend the day together. Gradually Bryan's affection seems to have been weaned away from his father — who was always, by 1887, "groaning, spitting and squabbling". The squabbling, he said, had gone on ever since he was "old enough to notice". "They always spoke politely before the servants but before me it was awful . . . obstinate and disagreeable" after Berridge's birth; before, they had been "on very good terms". Bryan had asked his mother why George was so disagreeable, and Alice's response was that he "was very much tried . . . I have not been very good to him." In July 1887 Bryan noted a temporary improvement in his parents' relationship, but in September his father went to London several times, and his mother said "my father was going to put her outside the door".

Poor Bryan, like so many children in similar circumstances, was torn between two parents whose differences he could scarcely begin to understand. At first loyal to his father, then encouraged to prefer Ames, there is a last hint that eventually he remained true to his father.

After the revelations of September 1887 there continued for three months all the legal paraphernalia for the preparation of the case. In October George had to prepare an account of his income to assess the alimony payable to the now separated Alice. This proved very difficult for him, as he had no accountant or manager; moreover "his head was dizzy and his memory bad at present". By October 22nd the solicitors learned that "creeping paralysis" was diminishing George's strength and a deposition became urgent. Throughout October Alice's movements were still being watched to provide further evidence of her misconduct.

On November 12th George requested the solicitor to come urgently to Hollingbourne as he wished to make a will as "my heart is all wrong" and he feared sudden death. In spite of Bryan's earlier resolve to "stick with his mother", on November 19th George had a letter from his son acknowledging his duty "to throw his fate in with me entirely" and saying that he had realised his father was right in "putting her away". By November 22nd George was planning to go to Spain as his health was declining daily. He expressed concern for that "poor little girl" Vivienne when she falls into her mother's hands. By November 25th George felt he could no longer put his nose out of doors without "a spasmodic affection of the lungs which almost stifles me", and was hoping to get to Biarritz, leaving his case to be fought in his absence. In early December he seemed rather better, then a telegram summoned Bryan from his school on account of his father's illness. The doctor's diagnosis was heart disease and dropsy.

On January 1st 1888 George's nephew Alured wrote to the solicitors that his uncle was lapsing into unconsciousness and increasing weakness; and on the 5th they received a telegram from Hollingbourne saying: "All over. Come directly."

George's life had come to an end. The Registrar of the Divorce Court was told "the Petitioner herein died on the 5th day of January instant whereby his Cause has abated."

Mary Thomas wrote in her diary: "A more miserably sad ending to an ambitious life could not be. Everything failed . . . certainly he died in good measure from a broken heart. Wonder what his despicable wife's feelings are now?"

Mrs Louisa Thomas, older, widowed, a grandmother, who perhaps knew there are always two sides to a story, commented more discreetly: "Mr Duppa passed away. Such a life of struggle and success, and disappointment and misery."

The Rest of the Story

SAVED at the eleventh hour from being the central figure in a scandalous divorce case, Alice was freed to marry the lover who was certainly the father of her daughter Vivienne, and probably of her third son, Berridge Greville. How *did* the "despicable wife" feel now? There would surely have been some remorse mixed with her relief. She had admitted to her son Bryan that she "had not been very good" to George Duppa, and the letters addressed to him as "Beastie" or "Peter" imply a playful and moderately amiable attitude on her part. She had seen no reason why they should not potter along together in a friendly way in spite of her affaire, and however disreputable such an attitude is, it is not that of a woman who wishes her husband dead.

However, it is unlikely that the year of formal mourning which passed between George's death and Alice's second marriage was a sad one. During that year she had to secure what legal rights she could as his widow. His last will, not surprisingly, made no mention of her. It also passed over Bryan, the obvious heir, in favour of a nephew, Richard Duppa Turbutt. Presumably Bryan did not seem to his father capable of managing a large, complex and not very prosperous estate, and received instead an annuity as much for his own sake as for the estate's. Berridge was not mentioned at all.

Alice's marriage to Major Ames took place on February 20th 1889, at the British Embassy in Paris, perhaps to avoid publicity at home. It was, however, reported in the *Maidstone and Kentish Journal* on February 26th.

The marriage of Mrs Duppa, eldest daughter of the late Sir Philip Miles and Lady Miles of Leigh Court, Somerset, and Major Ames, 1st Dragoon Guards, of the Hyde and Ayot St Lawrence, took place on Wednesday at the British Embassy in

170

Paris. The guests began to assemble at three o'clock, and the bride, who arrived accompanied by her mother at half past three, was given away by Mr Mansel Lewis, her brother-in-law. The bride's mother was dressed in a charming costume of *rose thé* to match the bride. The bride's dress consisted of a train of palest rose and *duchesse* satin, trimmed with old Venice point lace, *tablier* of old brocade in pink and gold, bonnet to match. She wore a superb necklace and *parure* of pearls and diamonds, the gift of the bridegroom. Mr Victor Ames was the best man, and Miss Leslie Catherwood attended the bride and held her bouquet. The Rev Howard Gill, Chaplain to the Embassy, performed the service.

Gerard's home at Ayot St Lawrence was now Alice's, and the couple had two more children, Lionel Gerard born in 1890, and Eve Marjorie, born in 1891. The Ames's house, Ayot House, is some distance from the centre of the attractive and still unspoiled village. Today, Ayot's houses, of many different periods, are scattered along winding lanes, or sequestered among shrub-bordered drives. There is a fine old inn, a post office and tea-shop, and of course the famous "Shaw's Corner", home of George Bernard Shaw, now the property of the National Trust. There are also two unusually interesting churches. The ancient church of St Lawrence, parts of which date from the twelfth century, is now a ruin, and covered with ivy. It did not fall into decay, but was deliberately attacked by the Lord of the Manor (Sir Lionel Lyde) in the 1770s, because it obstructed his view and he therefore decided to demolish it and build a new "classical" church elsewhere. He was foiled in his plan by the Bishop of Lincoln, but the church was never repaired. Lyde's new church is said to be a "very perfect example" of the Palladian style, having an open porch with four classical columns, and open pavilions, again with classical columns, flanking the main building. It is, to say the least, a most uncommon church to find in an English village.

The period after 1889 was, one hopes, a happy one for Alice. It is unfortunately just out of reach of living memory of even the oldest inhabitants of Ayot, though a few stories linger on. It is sad that there are no records relating to it, and even sadder is the known fact of the death of Gerard Ames in April 1899, in Paris, where he had been visiting his daughter Vivienne at her school. In the cool pale light of the Palladian church is a wall memorial tablet to Gerard Vivian Ames. His rather stern and soldierly face, with receding hair and a heavy moustache, confronts us uncompromisingly, but the epitaph reads: "To the dear memory of Lt Col Gerard Vivian Ames, 1st Royal Dragoons, Lord of the Manors of the Hyde and Ayot St Lawrence, who died in Paris, April 27th 1899, aged 46. Deeply regretted, and tenderly beloved. 'Grant us thy peace.' " But it is in the old church-yard, surrounded by sycamores and laurels, that Gerard's remains lie, below a carved stone cross which repeats the details of his death and adds "Omnia vincit amor". Alice and their son Lionel are also buried there.

What effect this tragedy had on Alice, we can but conjecture. She and Gerard had been married only ten years, she had suffered the tragic loss of both Archie and her young sister Violet in 1883, and her father, to whom she seems to have been attached, had died in 1888. Her religious beliefs, always ambiguous, may not have sustained her, but a month after his death she was able to reply to a letter of condolence received from Mrs Louisa Thomas. It is pleasing to think some degree of friendship survived between these two, and one would dearly love to know how much Mrs Thomas knew; but her diaries are the quintessence of discretion at all times.

Soon after Gerard's death Alice left the big house at Ayot and moved into the vacant Rectory. The living was in the gift of the Ames family, and Alice had a new rectory built, less attractive than the old one, being heavily Victorian, but comfortable and commodious nonetheless. It was this new rectory which, thanks to some typically Alicean machinations, became the home of George Bernard Shaw and his wife, and is now "Shaw's Corner". The story of how this came about was related to his wife (she was on holiday) by Shaw in a letter dated April 19th 1912.

We are safe here at Ayot for another eighteen months, it seems. The bishop would not hear of a rector who would not live in the Rectory . . . It looked like having to turn out. Mrs Ames, however, was equal to the occasion. She named a young curate named [Lane Claypon]. He rushed off to the bishop, who is a friend of his father. The bishop accorded an interview, but barred the subject of the rectory as finally disposed of. This being fully granted, Claypon said his father had suffered reverses. The bishop was full of concern. Claypon wanted to make a home for him in the rectory. The bishop was enchanted with his filial piety. The difficulty was that the father's lease of another house was not yet exhausted. The bishop deplored the fact. At last, when they were on thoroughly cordial terms, Claypon asked the bishop whether it would be all right for him to take on that big house all by himself. The bishop said that nothing could relieve him of that sacred obligation, and that he must be prepared to do so — say within eighteen months. Claypon rushed back to Ayot triumphant and danced a bacchanal with Mrs Ames, who is confident that the bishop will be translated in eighteen months to Essex. Anyway, we have time to breathe.

They continued to breathe there for the rest of their lives.

Many months after I began this story of Alice, when all the facts knowable seemed to be at hand, a completely unexpected bonus arrived in the shape of a previously unknown diary for the year 1908, written by Alice's youngest son, Lionel Gerard. Born a year after Alice's marriage to his father he reveals interesting glimpses of Alice, no longer the coquettish girl, nor the respected wife of the Squire, nor the disconsolate widow, but simply "Ma". Lionel's diary, written at the age of seventeen or eighteen, opens with him at Lathbury "cram college". Having disgraced himself there in various scrapes and horseplay, he was sent away, and was fortunate in gaining admission to the army college at Farnham which he found not much less boring. Capable of writing a grammatical sentence, he shows nothing of his mother's imaginative fluency of expression, and his diary is a trite record of studies, scrapes, betting on horses, pursuing beautiful actresses (so far as his very limited means allowed) and the occasional burst of horseplay which he designates as "no ordinary rag", frequently to be followed by "no ordinary row" with his tutors.

But the diary also reveals a happy rather robust family life, much enjoyed by Lionel when he could escape to Ayot. His older sister Vivienne and his younger sister Eve, with numerous friends and relatives, are seen at tennis, bicycling, walking, dancing and going to the London theatres, and of course "ragging". The impression is of an affectionate, noisy bunch of youngsters, in a period when the restraints of Victorianism were beginning to relax, in the halcyon days before the First World War, when a lot of fun and amusement could be had for relatively little money. Lionel writes more than once "my £1 due today but Ma never sent it". However, he saw Seymour Hicks, Lily Elsie, Irene Vanbrugh and other stars of the London stage. He stuck photographs of them in his diary, together with a few pictures of his beautiful sisters. Occasionally he managed to persuade some pretty young actress to go out with him — sometimes to Fuller's, where they enjoyed "no ordinary tea". The whole family seems to have been stage-struck. Vivienne, tall and striking, would, says Lionel, "love to go on the stage. Whereat Mother promptly and surely proceeded to sit on her. She would at once sever all links with the family and be disowned. Vivienne didn't want to go on the stage from the acting point of view, but to behave like all those common hussies, and show off her legs to admiring young men."

In June 1908, soon after beginning army college, Lionel fell ill and his mother was summoned. He was sufficiently alert to make the nurse "take down my picture gallery" — one envisages a frou-frou of young ladies with bare shoulders and frilly petticoats. On June 21st he was operated on for appendicitis, and "if I had not had the operation I should not have lived another 24 hours". "Ma" waited on him devotedly until July 9th, and he continued to have his wound dressed and enemas administered for some time after that, not being allowed to walk until August 2nd. As soon as possible he went to convalesce, first at home "under the big beech", then at Thornham in Norfolk, from where he visited his brother "Dups" — Berridge Greville Duppa, now married to a girl called Elsie. Lionel was fond of Dups, but whether he knew they were full brothers or thought of him as a half-brother is not known.

An interesting entry occurs on December 18th:

Lady Miles died this evening 8 o'clock quite suddenly. She had been in bed and she suddenly insisted upon walking across the room. Or rather getting up. The nurse protested but of course to no avail. She walked across the room to and collapsed into an armchair. She died without a word as soon as she sat down. Strangely enough, when the doctor came to see her, she told him she was going to die. Finding her quite well and her heart sound, he naturally replied "nonsense".

In 1904 Lady Miles — a widow since 1888 — had remarried. Her husband was a Dr John Nichols of St Louis, USA. He appears for a moment in Lionel's entry for December 27th.

Met Ma on her way back from the funeral. Poor Nichols was out of his mind with grief and was going on about slaying all the

domestic animals. Aunt May [Mabel, Alice's sister] had behaved
disgracefully because everything had been left to Nichols and
nothing to her. Ma was furious at her behaviour and so was Aunt
Edie.

The next entry contains another illuminating note.

An extraordinary change came over Ma after dinner. We all sat
round the fire and Ma actually joined in our conversation and we
all laughed and talked together. What a pity she is not always
like that.

This is at once puzzling and poignant. Clearly Alice was rarely
animated and happy. The brilliant spirits of her youth, the relative
tranquillity of the early years of her first marriage, and the stimulation
of her love affair with Gerard were no more. Perhaps, like Queen
Victoria, she spent her remaining years mourning for her beloved
husband; or perhaps the moral confusion, self-deception, unfulfilled
ambitions, disappointments and griefs of her chequered life had ended
by submerging her in clinical depression. She may have attempted to
give her life meaning by turning to theosophy: her will was to leave to
her sister Mabel "my theosophical library", which suggests that her
books on the subject were more than a casual collection. There are
also a few vague family recollections of a "guru" who was a house
companion (a male figure who looks Indian appears in one or two
faded photographs), and Lionel's diary describes her once as "meditating in the Holy of Holies".

Of Alice's other occupations in Ayot we know almost nothing. In
1988 she was just remembered by Mrs Harding as a shadowy,
reclusive figure living a withdrawn existence who bred dogs and
rarely got rid of them, so that she was always surrounded by crowds of
puppies. Mrs Harding thought that towards the end of her days she
made use of the barbiturate Veronal, which may have led to a
diminution of energy and awareness.

Alice lived on to reach her seventy-sixth year in 1926. Her son
Bryan married, but his only child died young; Berridge married but
had no child, and died before his mother in 1921. Vivienne married
and had a son, but Eve was left a childless widow. Lionel was
provided for by Gerard's will, and Alice's will distributed her money
and goods among her children, sisters and daughters-in-law. There

were three codicils revoking and altering bequests, the last of which, dated July 6th 1921, was witnessed by "George Bernard Shaw, author" and "Charlotte Frances Shaw, married woman", which suggests that Alice's next-door neighbours for twenty years had continued to be on fairly intimate terms with her.

Her jewellery, furs and pictures are scattered, their whereabouts unknown. Whether she continued to keep a diary steadily, or only intermittently, is also unknown. All we have are the notebooks recalling the brilliant years, as a sundial captures only the sunny hours. Her photograph albums still exist, from which some of the illustrations in this book have been taken. Alice the young matron appears languid, unsmiling and romantic, a truly suitable model for that never-was portrait by Greuze. And she is still unsmiling in later photographs, the full mouth almost pouting, the heavy-lidded eyes looking not at the camera but beyond it.

Her remains lie with Gerard's in the wild churchyard, among the moss-encrusted stones and the tall bird-loud trees. The inscription says only: "Also his wife Alice Catherine Ames, died 3rd April 1926, aged 76 years."

The grave is overgrown, the stone cross and kerbs stained with lichen; but in that peaceful place one seems to catch an echo of Alice's youthful voice murmuring her wish to be allowed to "lie under some grassy mound in the churchyard where I dreamed the sweetest dreams . . ."

GENEALOGIES

THE DUPPA FAMILY OF HOLLINGBOURNE HOUSE, KENT, to 1888

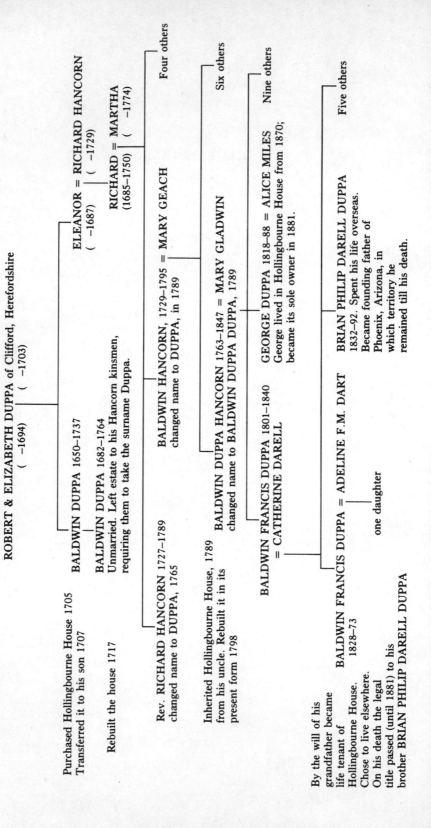

ROBERT & ELIZABETH DUPPA of Clifford, Herefordshire
(–1694) (–1703)

ELEANOR = RICHARD HANCORN
(–1687) (–1729)

RICHARD = MARTHA
(1685–1750) (–1774)

Four others

Purchased Hollingbourne House 1705
Transferred it to his son 1707

BALDWIN DUPPA 1650–1737

Rebuilt the house 1717

BALDWIN DUPPA 1682–1764
Unmarried. Left estate to his Hancorn kinsmen,
requiring them to take the surname Duppa.

BALDWIN HANCORN, 1729–1795 = MARY GEACH
changed name to DUPPA, in 1789

Six others

Rev. RICHARD HANCORN 1727–1789
changed name to DUPPA, 1765

Inherited Hollingbourne House, 1789
from his uncle. Rebuilt it in its
present form 1798

BALDWIN DUPPA HANCORN 1763–1847 = MARY GLADWIN
changed name to BALDWIN DUPPA DUPPA, 1789

Nine others

BALDWIN FRANCIS DUPPA 1801–1840
= CATHERINE DARELL

GEORGE DUPPA 1818–88 = ALICE MILES
George lived in Hollingbourne House from 1870;
became its sole owner in 1881.

BALDWIN FRANCIS DUPPA = ADELINE F.M. DART

one daughter

BALDWIN FRANCIS DUPPA
1828–73

By the will of his
grandfather became
life tenant of
Hollingbourne House.
Chose to live elsewhere.
On his death the legal
title passed (until 1881) to his
brother BRIAN PHILIP DARELL DUPPA

BRIAN PHILIP DARELL DUPPA
1832–92. Spent his life overseas.
Became founding father of
Phoenix, Arizona, in
which territory he
remained till his death.

Five others

THE MILES FAMILY OF LEIGH COURT, BRISTOL

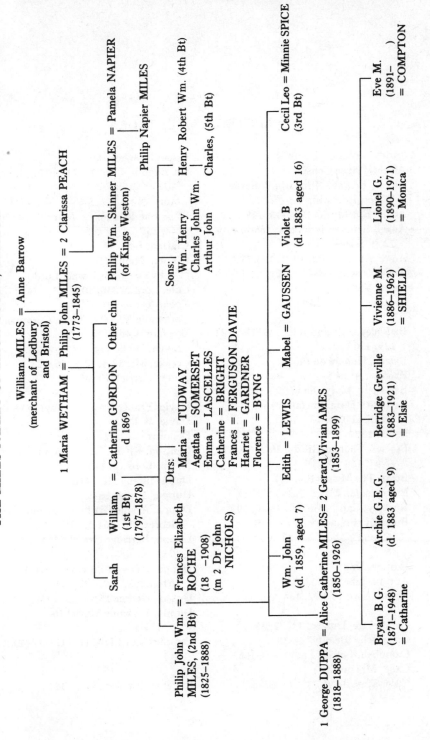

SELECTED NAMES INDEX